SOME BOYS

SOME BOYS

MICHAEL DAVIDSON

GMP

This edition first published in August 1988 by GMP Publishers Ltd,
P O Box 247, London N15 6RW.
Incorporating the author's own corrections as marked on his copy of the
original 1970 edition.
World copyright © 1970 and 1988 the estate of Michael Davidson.

Distributed in North America by Alyson Publications Inc.,
40 Plympton St, Boston, MA 02118.

British Library Cataloguing in Publication Data

Davidson, Michael
    Some boys.
    1. Great Britain. Journalism. Davidson,
    Michael, Biographies
    I. Title
    070'.92'4

    ISBN 0-85449-087-6

Printed and bound by Norhaven A/S, Viborg, Denmark

CONTENTS

MARRAKECH

THE CHLEUH is a southward looking man; from his home on the further slopes of the Atlas mountains or below in the Sous valley on the verge of the Sahara, the sun is forever in his eyes—from the moment it rises somewhere beyond the Algerian sands until it reaches the rim of the *moghreb el-aksa,* the extreme west, he is face to face with it more starkly, surely, than any other. His back is always to the north and from the vast reflecting wall of the Atlas he gazes from birth to death into the burning south. That, at least roughly, has been his historical destiny since the Chleuh people—they are more than a tribe—have been settled along the southern marches of Morocco.

And yet, in spite of all this ferocious sunshine, the Chleuh —who belong to a sept of the great Berber race of North Africa—are a fair-complexioned, slender, small-boned people, elegant and even feminine in their movements, with delicate and slightly womanish features. The milky-white cheeks of their sons are often capable of a maidenly blush; while the sexual ambiguities of their tribal dance, performed by the boys and ephebes, are renowned. In this dance the youths wear an ankle-length white garment, more feminine than masculine, and—especially relevant—a woman's belt; a girdle that no other North African male would dream of fastening round his waist; and the dance itself, executed to the beat of flute and tambour by twenty or more youths ranged in a circle, is a tremulous shuffling shimmy which we Westerners, most of us, would hail as a lovely send-up of a drag party. Yet what seems like an exercise in camp choreography in fact is a national tradition descended from a legendary past; the

7

equivocal appearance and androgynous vibrations of these apparently bisexual boys are symbols and emblems evolved by history. But symbols of what?

What is the ancestry of this curious *équivoque* which one discerns in the tradition of the Chleuh, and even in their emotional temperament (though I've never heard that they're any more prone to homosexual behaviour than any other North Africans—nor any less)? Whence comes this streak of femininity that seems to course through the generations of the Chleuh male—otherwise as masculine and vigorous as anybody? They are by nature a gentle people, farmers and foresters, tilling their terraces cut into the high mountain slopes, or their fertile fields by the river below, and living in small walled villages built in a style of which their great city of Taroudant is the noblest flower. I don't think the Chleuh, in the history of a half-continent's warlike people, have been specially prominent in war; they prefer a tranquil life. And, as I've said, their lives are sun-drenched day in, day out.

Can it be that the very sun has something to do with it? While unqualified to proffer any theories about cause and effect, I can certainly say from experience that solar exuberance and sexual liberality are widely to be found coincident. In those golden hot latitudes where the sun blazes long and strong and, one often feels, for ever, where the soft sultriness of the atmosphere and the liberating lightness of one's scanty clothes together work like a refreshing aphrodisiac—in those regions where the sun is really hot and seldom hidden except by night, there's a sexual laxity or tolerance—permissiveness is the modern word—which finds expression in almost any youth's perfect readiness to indulge his ever-brimming desires in whatever manner and with whichever sex he's offered. That this climatic permissiveness is widely recognized and respectably joked about is shown by that very old chestnut, recounted for at least half a century in London smoking-rooms and British officers' messes, about the Consul in Pernambuco. "You want woman? You want small girl? You want nice boy?" an important visitor, arriving in the city, is asked. "No, no," snaps the visitor testily, "I want the British Consul." Says the pimp: "That is difficult, but it can be arranged."

So the sun it may be; and even classical myth attributes to Apollo the introduction to humanity—or at any rate a principal share in it—of the male's love for a youth. Apollo, some ancient writers say, was the first god ever to love a member of his own sex and competed with the first mortal to do so, the poet Thamyris, for the affections of the lovely Hyacinthus—indeed there were two other rival suitors for the boy: Boreas and Zephyr, the North and West Winds. The latter was so enraged by Phoebus's apparent success that he caused the discus the boy was learning to throw to boomerang on to his own skull, killing him on the spot; and where Hyacinthus's blood fell, there sprang the flower. And although geographical purists may insist that this episode occurred in Sparta, a long way east of Morocco, it can't be denied that nowhere does Apollo's passionate eye stare with more fiery steadiness than upon the southern face of the Atlas mountain; and on those foothills undoubtedly the hyacinth grows.

The sun it may be; but the world's belt of perfervid sunshine is wide and broad, and there's no evidence that I know of that the Chleuh are more susceptible to unconventional seduction than anybody else. So the strange hermaphroditism of their dance and the hint of girlishness in their boys' demeanour remain unexplained, their causes hidden in the mists of antiquity.

Wrongly and deplorably, the city Arabs of Morocco—descendants, or claimants to descendance, from the original Arab invaders of the seventh and eighth centuries, largely living in the towns—are inclined, or used to be, to dub "Chleuh" any Berber-speaking people in a tone of slight denigration; in the same way, somewhat, as all Latins in the United States used to be called "dagos." Mustapha, my "Arab" boy-companion for three happy years of long ago, himself certainly of Berber ancestry, used to say, apologizing for the rusticity of some visitor, "Oh, he's just a Chleuh," when in fact the visitor was nothing of the sort. Was, I sometimes wondered, the quite wrongful taint of general disparagement often given by the Arabs to the name, to be traced to this semblance of effeminacy tucked into a corner of a manly and martial nation?

A note of apology here to the reader, before this sketch moves on towards its proper termination—about the tiresome and mechanical matter of transliteration. "Chleuh" is the

French way of rendering the native sound; the phonetic capabilities of English orthography being small, the word is impossible to reproduce in English—particularly as the final *h* is aspirated, like a Greek "breathing". In German one could write *Schlöh*, though that still doesn't sound the *h*: conventional transliteration from Arabic puts a dot underneath an aspirated *h*. In English perhaps one could write "Shlur"—pronouncing the *ur* as in "absurd" or "turd", and trying to remember the final *h*.

* * *

All visitors to Morocco, from travellers in the days of Leo Africanus to members of the present-day "package tours" and coach-tour "safaris" which the world's travel-agents organize, want to see Marrakech, the great red city in the south, capital of the Atlas barons. And there, the first place they go to is the *J'maa el-fna,* the vast piazza or "place of assembly", as the Arabic has it, which is the focal point of the people's footsteps and the scene of all the fun of the fair. An Islamic "fair", at any rate in Morocco, has a religious slant, or rather an occult or medico-magical one : nearly all the "shows" have a supernatural intention : the invocation of saint or demon for the purpose of curing disease, recovering stolen property, restoring a lost sheep or purse, reclaiming an adulterous husband, or some similar reasonable need. All these miracles are performed by the disciples of certain saints or the members of certain sects who've been endowed with special powers over *djinn* or other spectral beings—who are, in fact, sorcerers. Thus the Aissaoui, through their sympathy with snakes, can influence certain potent *djinn*; the Ouled Sidi Khalifa can, through the immense disc of their thrumming drums, into which the drummers whisper as their hands beat out an evocative rhythm, call up from the netherworld the most remarkable demons, capable of solving all sorts of useful domestic problems; which they do after throwing their supplicants into trance-inducing jig, a hysteria something like that which the modern pop-fans of the West attain through the mesmeric rhythm of their idols. I suppose that the Chleuh dance too has some sacramental or animistic meaning, though I don't know what it is; but no like ceremonial rite of such antiquity, in Morocco, can be without some amount of power for good or ill.

Nor do I know whether the Chleuh dance has joined so many other old traditionalist popular fantasies—all cherished by the ordinary, illiterate folk and all harmless—beneath the ban of the new nationalist puritanism. When I revisited Morocco some five years ago I found that the eager reformist hyperchauvinistic government of King Hassan, bent upon presenting to the world a modern, go-ahead, modish "image" no matter how wretched the common people beneath it might be, was suppressing all the popular customs that smacked of superstition or heresy; an outward show of Islamic conformity was officially required, while any folklorist unorthodoxies, no matter how picturesque the tourists might find them, were made illegal. On the common people, the effect was rather the same as if in America baseball were banned as being degrading to the national "image"; but in Morocco the common people don't count.

I'm perfectly sure that the new puritanism will have banned a very specialized edition of the Chleuh dance, one arranged for a very special audience. It was in Marrakech that this took place; and I haven't been in Marrakech since some years before the French resigned the Moroccan power to the Moroccans—and in those days there was a greater permissiveness, under the French, than there is today. I think if one asked the hall porter of the Mamounia Hotel, today, about seeing this *special* Chleuh dance, he'd shake his head and sorrowfully say he couldn't help—poor fellow, he'd be losing a tip. . . .

But in those old days almost any hotel porter, approached confidentially, would be willing, for a consideration, to give equally confidential instructions to a cab-driver. The last time I saw this spectacle was in 1947, and it was the very grand-looking commissionaire of the Mamounia who helped me—at a time when Winston Churchill was a visitor inside, recovering from an illness. I whispered to the porter *"les gosses chleuhs,"* and passed him a whopping tip. He called up the nearest cabby and whispered the same three words; and off we drove.

As I remember it now, the place inside looked rather like what in England is called a "village hall"; where jumble-sales are held and parochial concerts presented. It was quite small, and the greater part of one half was filled with a stage, which was brightly lit up by stark electric lamps. There was no curtain. We sat—I'd gone with a friend—on one of a couple of benches in front of the platform; on the floor behind were a few rush sleeping mats, rather dingy and dirty now, but still displaying those delightfully coloured geometrical patterns which the mountain Berbers plait and dye from the wild dwarf palm and home-grown pigments. The impresario was a skinny, middle-aged city Arab, with a meagre beard. He wore a red fez and shabby sky-blue *djellaba* and, unlike most Arab businessmen, wasn't interested in bargaining : either we paid what he asked, or we didn't come in. He knew we'd come in, and therefore pay : he knew his public. I could certainly see his point. That evening we were the only customers, and I suppose on many evenings no audience turned up at all. We paid about ten dollars each (ten dollars twenty years ago) for about twenty minutes' show—any services provided after the show were charged for like "extras" on a hotel bill. But I felt that the ten dollars were well spent : not solely because the spectacle was one of rare interest, and excitingly erotic, but also because it was unique and, in a sense, historically unrepeatable; nowhere else in the world and probably never again in time would one see this barefaced, and barebottomed, version of the strange and cryptic Chleuh dance.

There were seven or eight boys and they ranged in age, judging by appearance, from about seventeen down to eleven. They filed in on to the stage from a side door, the smallest boy first, and stood for a moment facing the "audience"—us two—in a row : "sized" like soldiers, tallest on the left, shortest on the right; so that they seemed evenly stepped downwards like a set of organpipes. They were all wearing long white cotton gowns, belted at the waist. Then the impresario started to thrum out a rhythm on a tambour of stretched goatskin, and a concerted tremor, like a breeze through a field of corn, shivered through the rank of angel-robed boys; their bare feet began to whisper and sigh over the boards of the stage in a strange sort of static shuffle, without their shifting position; their bodies, beneath the thin stuff of their garments, were seized in a kind of symmetrical paroxysm of trembling undulation and their cropped black-haired heads nodded and jerked as if scanning an unending series of hexameters; half-a-dozen or more long lush black eyelashes fluttered and ogled like feathered fans. I looked at those faces, pale as parchment most of them, with high cheek bones and small Berber noses delicate as a lamb's, and lips full of warmth and youngness : beautiful faces, in the way that some masks are beautiful; cold, immobile expressions without feeling, like conventional marbles—if hunger or exhaustion seemed to be the sensations uppermost behind these wan childish cheeks, it was just one's guess. Only their dark liquid eyes were alight : but their fire reached beyond the walls of this room—like the eyes of boys in school who aren't listening to the lesson.

There was something hieratic about them; a hint of sacerdotal virginity in the long flowing folds of their robes, like albs, with high chaste necks buttoned at the throat, and their close-cropped monkish heads; one might have imagined them to be a group of cloistered novices performing some ritual of spiritual initiation. And then suddenly the smallest boy at the end of the descending scale, as if in answer to a quickening of the drummer's beat, unbuckled the woman's girdle from his waist and, with a deft sleight-of-hand that one scarcely noticed, threw off his single long garment and continued the dance as naked as he was born, without the slightest variation in the tempo of his undulations—undulations which now, of course, could be watched in every flexion of his muscles and each tremor of his flesh. And then the rest followed suit : first, the next to him in size and place; and then his slightly taller neighbour; and so on until all seven or eight of them were stark naked and still dancing with the same mechanical impassivity, as if it were all the same to them whether they had clothes on or none. Now, in the harsh lights on the stage, one could see every detail of their bodies, though still no more of the hearts and minds within than one could before; they were Muslim, of course, these Chleuh boys, and so all were circumcized (in the Moroccan *bled*, or countryside, circumcision is done generally at about eight or nine years old) and those who had reached puberty and beyond, obedient to the Koranic rule, had shaved any hair they may have had around their genitals or in the armpits; though the tallest, who must have been seventeen at least, had already allowed, again in accordance with Islamic practice, the dark down on his upper lip and cheeks to sprout into an untidy fluff. Of course, I was fascinated by the sight of this graded rank of lean, quivering nudity; and a miscellany of leaping genitalia, from tiny to immense, each as unique among the rest as its owner's countenance in a crowd. Their bodies were beautiful—for young creatures are always beautiful: in spite of ribs which pressed too sharply against such puny skin, in spite of shoulderblades like ploughshares and harrowingly thin thighs; one watched these poor bodies with a pang of guilt. They shimmied and shuffled and their slim long fingers dangled against their buttocks; a row of drowsy penises bobbed and frolicked as involuntarily as corks being juggled by the jets of a fountain, and a row of sad blank faces were as cold and colourless as moons. The spectacle was spell-binding, yet chilling too in the heart. . . .

Now the drum again seemed to miss a beat and change to a more urgent measure; and all the boys did a left-turn, so that they faced into single file, with the smallest in the lead. Slowly they began to advance, round and round the small stage in a circle; then speed imperceptibly increased, like a boat gathering way—a shuffling walk slid into a jog-trot and thence into a run: and then they were galloping round like an unruly riding-school, each trying to gain on the other—and the next moment they'd all seized their cocks in their hands and, making obscene thrusting leaps forward, each was mimicking attempts to rape the boy ahead of him: thus the oldest and tallest of them, while apparently in hot pursuit of the boy next to him in size, seemed at the same time to be fleeing from the baby of the lot—who, firmly gripping his tiny pintle in his right hand, was scampering after the broad bottom of a youth twice his own height.

And there the show ended. The throbbing of the drum abruptly broke off like church bells stopping in the middle of a peal; the impresario, looking scraggier and more sour-faced than before, wiped his forehead with a sleeve, pushing back a fez whose felt rim was stained dark with sweat. The boys picked up their garments, and slouched wearily off stage. The impresario then told us we could choose any of the boys we fancied—there'd be an extra fee for that, plus any gift we liked to give the boy, and a small charge for the use of a mat. . . . We declined this offer; but we did manage to find the boys and give them some money for sharing among themselves. Don't let the Master of the Drum get it, we whispered to them—and to this day I've been praying that the impresario didn't grab that money from them.

Looked at with the gluttonous eye of a Trimalchio, or the brutal one of his emperor, it was an amusing show; and my eye was little less sensual, little less vicious, than theirs. But it left a very nasty taste in my mouth. I suppose it was no more squalid, mean and perverted (in the wider sense) than any of thousands of furtive bordellos hidden about the world, where boys, little girls or pitiful and hopeless women are used to pay the rent of hundreds of madams, male and female. In those days there was tragic poverty in a city like Marrakech: starved and homeless boys begged and slept in the gutters. At least, some may argue, these dancing boys were being fed, even if meanly. Yes, perhaps. . . . Anyway, prostitution's never been a trade I would recommend to any child of mine, except possibly as a sideline, an *esercizio secondario,* like marrying for money. . . .

GENEVA

It SEEMS odd when I think of it now—that this very year, the year in which I'm writing, François would be fifty-six years old, or perhaps fifty-seven. For these things happened just four decades ago, in 1928, when he was sixteen; and when I see him in my mind's eye, which I often do, as plainly as if it were yesterday, it's like looking at a very old-fashioned photograph: I see him wearing what in those days were called "plus-fours", breeches bunched below the knee over long stockings; and an old-fashioned short haircut, with a forelock brushed upwards in front like a cock's comb. Even his face seems old-fashioned, like the faces in old school or college groups, looked at forty or fifty years on.

An easygoing, jolly face: not conventionally handsome and certainly not plain; laughing grey eyes with glints of gold in them, like quartz, and a broad, short nose with big nostrils that he loved to fill with the clean, cold air of the high mountains he delighted in. *"Là-haut sûr la montagne . . ."*— I can hear him singing still his favourite alpine song in that strong boyish baritone, clear and resonant over the silent snowy slopes. How he loved singing! . . . He had wonderful teeth, white and strong as an animal's and a mouth like two pigs of one of those scarlet blood-oranges one sees cut in half on Italian fruit-stalls: full, red, juicy lips that gave his whole face a look of sensuality. He was tall, though still boyishly slight; and much climbing had given him muscles like steel springs.

François had the strength and agiltiy and aptitude for high altitudes of a mountain goat. He had the lusts of a goat too; there was nobody he wouldn't fuck, or at least have some sort of sex with, if he got the chance. He used to boast to me that when he was fourteen he'd seduced his younger sister, aged twelve; and kept it up with the sister for nearly a year, until she went off to be a maidservant in some hotel at Lausanne. It was he who took me to Rosetta's bar, in a small side street near the Rhone. Rosetta was a limping old woman with a splendid Roman face and one leg shorter than the other: her singing was as histrionic as her dramatic features and her much-beribboned guitar—in a voice that would have filled the Scala she sang the Italian songs of that early fascist era—"La Giovinezza" was always in demand—and her small shabby bar was always crowded with people from the fringes of the Geneva underworld. François used to assure me that he had slept a whole night with Rosetta and had enjoyed it very much. Perhaps that was true; I preferred to think it wasn't.

That was a time when all the idealists' hopes, and all the politicians' cynicism, were poured into the new League of Nations, and enormous sums of dedicated money poured into its grandiose buildings in Geneva; and when Stresemann and Briand, over huge mugs of German beer at the Brasserie Gambrinus, might, if they'd been left alone by the Allied politicians, have devised a real European peace. It was a time, too, when the League and its ancillaries were offering a multitude of well-paid and nicely puffed-up jobs to the middle-class unemployed of Europe—the new international bureacracy was coming into being. I got one of the humbler of these jobs, and that's how I found myself in Geneva in 1928. One consequence, therefore, of the creation of the League of Nations was my meeting one night in the Rue des Alpes with François.

The Rue des Alpes, in those days, had tram-lines running down it and was a principal street between the railway station and the port, whence the steamers set out for points along both the Swiss and the French coasts of the Lake. Half way down the hill, in the middle of the road, stood a shelter for waiting tram passengers: a commodious structure of masonry with a kiosk open deep into the night, where drinks and snacks could be bought. It was, in fact, a place round which various kinds of night-birds used to congregate—not only "birds" in the modern sense, but also local layabouts and, often, young hikers from Germany who, hoping to find work, were first of all looking for food and bed. It was a good spot for making friends—or, better put, for a pickup.

Here too, late at night, waited the adventurous, anarchic adolescents who, unripe yet for grown-up night life, couldn't bear to cut experience short by going to bed; who, held like moths by the bright lights, hung on hour after hour on the chance of something exciting happening. François was like that—always waiting for a thrill; and it was at that noctiva-gant tram-stop that I met him. François had a key to his grandmother's back-street apartment, which he used merely as lodging and larder—although, as I found, there was an essential attachment, an umbilical affection, which held the two together, the old woman and her only surviving descen-dant, even though they were scarcely on speaking terms. (He couldn't remember either of his parents : what had hap-pened to them he wasn't quite sure.) But "home"—I don't think he'd ever known one : it wasn't "home" at his grand-mother's. "Up there," he'd say to me, pointing to the shining white Alpine skyline. "That's where I feel at home. Above the snow-line—my home's there." And when he looked up like that towards the distant mountains, the hard, laughing glint in his eyes seemed to soften.

François despised people who couldn't look after themselves; he used to say that if he couldn't find what labouring jobs he wanted, he'd take to burglary—he could never whine or fiddle for a living, he'd declare, or sell shoe laces shivering in the cold. He was a hefty boy, and enjoyed hefty work. When, that first night, we went to a brasserie and ate a plate of *fondu* each he wanted to pay; and it was he who bought, ahead of me, the wine we took back to my apartment just off the Rue des Alpes. And while we drank the wine he sang : those mountaineering songs whose words or tune or both seemed to turn the rather cynical jollity of his expression into something like happiness—

> *Là haut sûr la montagne.* . . .
> . . . . *c'était un vieux chalet.* . . .

—this was the song he loved best, though there were other French songs; and one famous one in German he used to try —but, French, as he put it, being the tongue he was born with, German didn't come comfortably :

Auf der Alpe regt ein Haus
Drûben über 's Tal hinaus. . . .

But it was "up there" that he was always singing or humming: the term "là-haut" had for him a mystical value. Sometimes, during our times together, I'd suddenly ask: "Where'd you like to be now?". He'd always answer: "Là-haut"; and he'd look out into the high distance. Nearly every weekend, weather permitting, he'd go off, generally by himself, to do some old favourite climb or some exciting new one; he spent all his spare money on fares and provisions, or on keeping his boots in good order.

That night—and many other nights too—we slept in the same bed, and only spent some of the time sleeping. He was always ready for anything, and hugely enjoyed any kind of sensuality; and he gave me, too, a kind of rollicking affection, as if it were a big joke. And yet, loyal and fond as he always was, I often had the feeling he would just as soon be doing whatever it was we were doing with almost anybody else. His mind, or at least his heart, seemed always elsewhere—*là-haut*, I supposed, in that glittering distilled solitude which was his heaven. Naked, he could have been a model for some sculptor's "athlete"; yet, because of the ridiculously narrow focus of my own sexual nature, he wasn't really my type—too big and brawny, for all his sinewy grace: too mature. Nevertheless, bewitched by his charm and gusto and the warmth of his high-spirited friendliness—and especially, I think, by his *uniqueness*—I was instantly infatuated.

Looking at him, listening to him, fascinated by him, I felt something of Byron in him: even his face, from its magical charm, acquired a sort of byronic beauty; and I could feel the same rumbustious enjoyment of laughter and singing and robust pleasure—with none of Byron's flaring temper, moodiness or sullen ill-manners. And there was too this sexual catholicity, this zest for everything, including incest. . . .

Soon he was spending nearly every evening with me as a matter of course: we'd go to some brasserie where there was music—French, German or Italian; and François, after two or three *décis* of wine, would add his rich boy's baritone to their songs and sometimes get them to accompany him in his own. Or we would spend a long and hectic evening at

Rosetta's; and next morning I'd leave hungover for my office long after he had blithely gone off to his labouring job.

Some Saturdays, when we were both free and there was a warm spring sun, we walked northwards along the bank of the Rhone to a small modest restaurant which, almost outside the confines of the town, seemed from the wall of its *terrasse* to hang right over the swift flow of the river. Here we'd eat trout or roast duck and drink a great deal of the *fendant* of Vallais, a pale golden wine, clean and clear and sharp as crystal : free of acid but deceptively light—after two or three glasses, one's every word was witty. We'd watch the great birds of prey, some fish-eating eagle or falcon, glide on a huge span of wing above the current and suddenly drop to the surface for a snatch. And then we'd walk back a little uproariously, along the river bank, François' singing accompanied by a good deal of histrionic gesture, and his voice echoing back from the buildings across the water. . . .

And soon what I'd been dreading would happen, did; he began insisting that I must come climbing with him—next weekend, the weekend after that, the first fine weekend, we would go : he would take me up on the Saturday to a "refuge" where we'd sleep; and at crack of dawn we'd be on our way up, up—*là haut* . . . up beyond the snowline. I told him I was no mountaineer, that I'd done no climbing, that I'd only be a nuisance to him, that I hadn't got the right boots or anything. . . . It didn't matter what I said; he wouldn't listen to any objections : the more he talked the keener he became—now all his happiness, all his pleasure, depended on his leading me up, on his showing me *his* mountains. I knew I wouldn't be able to disappoint him; and I knew I was too much of a coward to tell him I was *frightened* of mountains, that I *hated* heights, that I was a victim of vertigo and couldn't even look out of a second floor window without feeling dizzy.

His heart was set on taking me up some beastly mountain; soon he was talking about our expedition every evening, making plans, working out routes. I told him I was such an ass about climbing that I'd be a disgrace to him and spoil it all by making him ashamed of me. But he wouldn't listen; and said he'd take me on a very easy little ascent—just a lazy walk up, he said, that any child or old woman could manage.

I gave in, of course; but not before making one more protest. "I'm not going to spend money on a special outfit," I said, "boots and so on. And I can't go as I am, can I?" Yes I could, he snapped back, just as I was—hadn't I ever gone up an ordinary hill path before? And I'd be so *happy* up there, he begged—he wanted *so much* to show me what it was like up there—*là-haut*; Oh, *how* could I want to spoil it all for him? When he spoke like that, his grey glinting eyes seemed to flood with excitement. He was right: how *could* I . . . ?

We settled for the coming Saturday, if the weather allowed; and when the morning came we shouldered our rucksacks, full of food and wine and topped with blankets for the night. On the way through the town I stopped at a tobacconist's just taking down the shutters—I wanted enough cigarettes for myself. François despised my smoking—he would never touch a cigarette. "Smoke in your chest up there is like a charcoal stove in a shut-up room," he used to say. "Smoking, you can't breathe the clean air up there."

We went over to the French side of the border—I can't remember now whether we took a bus or crossed the lake by boat. It was a brilliant autumn morning of sharp air and sunlight—there was already snow well down the slopes ahead of us. We spent most of that day walking comfortably, climbing higher and higher; when I looked back over the lake, the steamers were mere specks, like ships seen from a high-flying plane. This is easy, I thought to myself—what had I been worrying about? François padded ahead as lightly as a mountain bear, and his singing seemed to grow in volume with every degree of altitude.

By the time we reached the resthouse, the air felt near freezing. Inside, we found a few others there already; before long, what with warmth and food and an exquisite exhaustion medicated with plenty of drink, I had become an enthusiastic mountaineer. This is the life for me, I thought! And the more wine I drank, the more melodious the singing of several songs at once seemed. And pure happiness came when François, the rest having warbled themselves into a torpor, could sing alone: *"Là-haut, sûr la montagne. . . ."*

I whispered to him: "We can't sleep together. . . ."

"Of course we can!" he said almost angrily. *"Mais bien sûr—je m'en fous des autres!"* What indeed did he care about the others? When François was excited and happy, he didn't care two cents what the whole world thought of him.

We couldn't take our clothes off; but we lay tightly close under our two blankets; and his kisses, up there on the mountain side, seemed to have more behind them than I'd known before. It was the mountain, I think, that he was kissing. . . .

And I had drunk far too much wine. I was to realize that again next morning.

*　　　*　　　*

It still seemed fairly easy going next day; though I was feeling hungover and nervy, and my heart was thumping a bit. But I kept going, determined to earn his approval—or anyway escape his jeers. There was still something of a path, with a good deal of scrambling up what seemed some pretty steep places—but I thanked heaven I could still look back without feeling dizzy. We came to snow, sparkling like tinsel under the sun; and the sparse trees were like frosted fretwork. Then all at once I was aware of a thing I'd never really thought of before—an absolute soundlessness, so extraordinary that it was almost as assertive as noise : at ordinary earthly levels there's always some sound in silence—the tiny ignored notes of birds, the rustling in the undergrowth; but here in this unearthly world there was *nothing* : we were beyond the bird level—we were in a bloodless, bodiless, abstract world where nothing lived but ourselves : I felt like a trespasser in some exquisite preserve of refrigerated death. Our little petty human voices sounded sacrilegious—until suddenly the whole mountain, the whole of heaven, became filled with François's singing, which seemed to roll for ever and unending over the snow and up to the peaks above and to have a purity of sound which I felt I'd never heard in a voice before. *"Là-haut, sûr la montagne,"* he sang, *". . . c'était un vieux chalet. . . ."* The sun was blazing down now, hot as in summer; and suddenly he began to tear his clothes off, even his boots and stockings; and then he was prancing and dancing in the snow, stark naked : shouting and singing, leaping and pirouetting, like a gloriously crazed satyr. Next minute he was rolling in the snow, burying himself under it, pulling handfuls of it over his whole body like a child burrowing in the sand at the seaside. I felt quite mad : the sparkling cold loveliness of this suspended world, the deathly soundlessness except for his echoing and empyreal melody, the stainless beauty of that perfect prancing nude, capering ecstatically in the snow in a kind of Bacchic, yet immaculate, rapture—it was enough to drive a man made of plumduff dotty. It was as if we'd suddenly reached Olympus, instead of a minor mountain in the neighbourhood of Mont Blanc—and he there, the possessor of that divinely white body, was an immortal, one of the gods— perhaps Dionysus, the boy god himself. Later, when I felt fairly sane again, and when François had put on his clothes and we were plodding upward through the snow, the ground rising ever more steeply, I thought that really I'd always sensed something of the nature of Pan in him, something half divine and half demonic : something fantastic that seemed to make him more than mortal—immortal in fact. It was, anyway, quite absurd to connect a being so vibrant and vital, a creature so manifestly akin to the sun and the stars and the firmament, with death or even the dismal approach to it : how could a boy so joyously and radiantly young even grow older?

The ascent, for me at least, was becoming difficult; and suddenly we came to what surely must be a full stop : there was obviously no getting up the sheer, flat wall of rock as high as a good-sized house at whose foot we had arrived.

"Well, what do we do now?" I asked. "You won't get me up there."

It's easy, he said : you just follow me.

"Mais, dis-donc, mon petit, ne blagues pas, toi! C'est une muraille"—une muraille, I repeated, a bloody great wall as tall as a prison.

He looked at me as if I were a sulky child. *"Pas de bêtise—* you've got handholds and footholds all the way up, easy as walking up a ladder. Simply watch me and you can't go wrong. Why, an old woman could climb this !" And he started up, climbing patiently, in slow motion, so to speak; carefully showing me every move and looking back to make sure that my fingers and feet were exactly following his. It was then, of course, that my hangover came back to me : I began to sweat, and feel slightly sick; and I knew that if I looked down for an instant I'd be stuck. François was infinitely unselfish and forbearing : not nagging at me, nor laughing; but gently, gently, advising and encouraging. In this way we arrived about halfway up, or a bit more : I suppose I had some ten feet yet to go above me, and a twenty-foot drop below. And suddenly I knew I'd had it : the climb hadn't become any more difficult—I simply couldn't move, up or down. I wanted to be sick; my tongue felt twice its size and horribly dry.

"François," I called, or tried to call—my voice seemed to have seized up—"*je n'en peux plus.* I can't do any more." He looked down at me expertly, weighing the situation : "Go down then, if you can't come up. Go down the way we came." I shook my head, gazing steadily upwards : I knew if I looked down I should fall. "Stay where you are then," commanded François, "and don't move. Stay just as you are till I come back." He seemed to run up the face of the "muraille" like a cat, and vanished over the cliff-edge at the top.

I don't know how long he was gone : it seemed eternity. My fingers were hooked—the most feeble, brittle, of grappling irons—into two tiny crevices; the tip of my toes perched on ledges that felt more and more tiny every instant. I still wanted to be sick; and I had a feeling I wouldn't be able to swallow next time I wanted to. Even at this distance of time I can remember almost every detail of those minutes of terror, waiting for François's return. I kept my head tilted upwards —partly because I was terrified of looking downwards, even by mistake; and partly because all existence and the world's whole destiny seemed to depend on my first glimpse of François' face peering over. I could feel the strength running out of fingers and toes like blood out of an artery—I *knew* I couldn't hang on much more, and that my only hope was to put every ounce of my consciousness into my hands and feet, to play a game of *willing* that they kept hanging on.

And then François came, with a rope—God knows where he'd got it : but just then, to me, François was God. He came down in seconds, and fastened the rope round me; then he was up top again, and hauling; and with this blessed, this divine, support I could help myself up by ledge and hand-hold.

At the top I was sick. "I'm sorry—but I told you I would let you down. I'm sorry I've disgraced you. Now I'm going to do worse—I'm going back to the resthouse." He showed me where the refuge stood away below us, and how to take the long way round to get down to it. Then he went striding off through the snow again towards the craggy pinnacle he was bent on climbing that day ("it's a child's climb," he'd told me). I hung about through the afternoon, waiting for him and feeling what a worm I was—I had let François down. Towards evening he came back; I could see he was happy in himself—the happiness of one who'd done what he'd set out to do.

"I'm sorry, François," I said again as we walked down; "but *la muraille* made me ill: it nearly killed me." He shrugged: "You didn't try."

We reached Geneva late that night, and after a silent supper went to bed. He was healthily tired, content with his own exertions, and told me to shut up about *"la muraille,"* as I called it—I had nightmares about it.

The memory of my terror and my silliness, clinging that day to the face of "la muraille," has often given me a nightmare in these last forty years. But within a few days of that unlucky weekend, we were both treating my experiment in mountaineering as a joke; and we were both referring to the whole expedition, and to that cliff of rock, as *"la muraille"*; and even the two or three boys he called *"mes copains"*—he had no close friends—got into the habit of calling the spot *"la muraille."* A week or two later I had to go to Berlin where I stayed a month or so; I sent François three or four picture-postcards, and gave him an address; but no word came from him. No word ever came from him again.

He knew what day I'd be back: I thought he would be sure to come that same evening—I even hoped he might be at the station to meet me: it would have been so like him to work out the trains from Berlin and the connection from Basle. But he didn't come at all. For several days he didn't come, and I began to worry a lot. After nearly a week I made up my mind to track down the grandmother's apartment, although he had never allowed me to go near it. But that evening, in the rue des Alpes, as I was passing the tram stop where I'd first met him, I ran into two of the *copains*.

"Where's François?" I asked, "I haven't seen him." They looked at their feet, and took a long time over lighting cigarettes, and shuffled about as sheepishly as young people do who aren't certain of their ground. *"Tiens*—you don't know—?"

"Don't know what? What is it—?"

"You haven't heard—the accident—?"

If I hurried them, I felt, if I wasn't very careful, I'd start screaming out loud. "Accident? What—what happened?"

"He'd gone to help somebody: he was roping somebody up and somehow—I don't know just what happened—something gave, and François was pulled over."

I couldn't speak. I could only wait for the finish of the story. They puffed laboriously at their cigarettes, and looked everywhere but at me.

"His neck was broken. At the bottom of *la muraille*."

*   *   *

Now, so often, forty years after, I hear that echoing voice, *"Là-haut, sûr la montagne. . . ."* and I'm haunted by the stainless beauty of that perfect prancing body in the snow; and I remember asking myself how a boy so joyously and radiantly *young*, could ever grow older. . . .

LAHORE

AFTER A heavy Indian lunch, of the sort which both turns the thoughts towards erotic fancy and at the same time annuls the power of thought, I sat in the shuttered room of the Lahore hotel and drowsily watched the great blades of the ceiling-fan jerking round like the reluctant propeller of an aircraft.

It was one of the massive wooden rooms that one found in the splendid old Indian hotels of colonial days : solid, easy-going, subservient; a vaguely baronial mixture of saddle-brown and crimson and a ritual oblation to the dignity and the comfort of the British Raj; it was also, in the same tradition and for the same reasons, a bungalow-like "annexe," having its own front door and thus giving its occupant complete privacy and independence of the main entrance.

The light in the room was like the deep shadow beneath a huge old English oak in full leaf : it pleasantly reminded one of the blinding burning white sunshine outside. The furniture was austere and simple; but as solid and reliable and sensible as most of the officers and functionaries who used it. There was no real bath or shower; in a flagged alcove stood an upturned washtub over which towards evening "bearer" and "cleaner" would busy themselves with cans of hot water so that the sahib might bathe before dressing for dinner. I remember the room, and that afternoon, perfectly well, even after all these years—the State of Pakistan was still blood-stained and brand-new, and only a few weeks earlier the dusty street outside the hotel had still been strewn with the corpses of Sikhs and Hindus killed in the crazed religious slaughter of two decades ago. I remember the room with especial clarity because that after-luncheon somnolence was interrupted by one of those fulminant sexual fortuities which burst one's heart with their unexpectedness and yet, afterwards, seem so absolutely natural and inevitable and *right* that once again one's belief in the Fates and predestination is restored. The Fates, when they mapped out their myriad human courses, devised a great deal of ingenious mischief; but they also dotted them with patches of intoxicating bliss. The sexual memory can be astonishingly enduring : the imprint of some erotic image from the past stays clearly in the mind's eye long after the circumstances have faded; details of genitalia are sometimes remembered when the face has long been forgotten—the recollection of some fortuitous fumble-and-tumble lasts on quite absurdly into a future until one's asking oneself where on earth it can have happened? The photographic memory seems to be furnished with an emulsion more sensitive to erotic phenomena than to ordinary concerns that don't whet this particular appetite : this is surely a natural fact which must be plain to anybody, even a bishop, who closely examines the working of his memory—a truth that is Nature's answer to St. Paul and others like him who worry about the purity of other people's minds. It seems to me that the natural preferences of the human memory, which are the memory's choice not the memorizer's, present a stronger argument than St. Paul's, which is the derivative of personal prejudice. Or is the memory's habit of storing away pictures of sensual delight merely evidence of original sin?

This is why, I suppose, the memory of that curious Lahore afternoon has lasted so exactly all these years : fresh and vivid after twenty years and in spite of the sombreness of that shadowed bungalow, veiled against the violence of the sun outside. I tried to read with the not very serious idea of escaping from the sexual daydreams that kept pleasantly but unpromisingly crawling into my mind; but the wide, slow-whirling propeller in the ceiling, besides swirling the air round in a circle immediately beneath its blades, blew the pages of the newspaper about unmanageably—while outside the circle, where the paper stayed comfortably still, the stagnant air was unendurably hot : I could feel the trickling sweat on my ribs. So I simply sprawled under the lumbering fan, listening to the faint squeak of its jerking revolutions, and allowing my daydreams to tantalize as much as they wanted.

But a sudden knock on the wooden door scattered the daydreams, it was so unexpected: who could be knocking at this time of day? The hotel bearers wouldn't think of disturbing a visitor's after-lunch nap unless there were a special reason—perhaps a cable had arrived for me? I'd been sitting half naked; I pulled on a bush-shirt for form's sake, and opened the door on to the blinding sunshine.

*   *   *

His colour was a light bay: his skin had a young sheen like a well-groomed horse's coat: but at first sight, against the brazen glare of the afternoon sky, he looked dark—as one's own hand, held up, looks black against the light. Beneath a dirty old floppy linen hat, of the kind English children used to wear in summer, locks of lank, dank sable hair hung over his eyes: immense black eyes with yellowish whites peeped between tufts of hair like an animal's peering through foliage —but unlike an animal's, there was neither threat nor fear in them; only speculation and, I thought, a hope of friendliness. His age must have been thirteen or fourteen; he wore a cotton shirt with its tails hanging over a pair of dust-coloured shorts and broken leather sandals. He was carrying under one arm a small black valise like a very old-fashioned doctor's bag.

"For orphanage, please," he said, and began opening the old brass clasps of the bag. I looked at his pale-dark face, the small, tender face, pert yet sweet, and the great soft eyes through the black locks. "Come in," I said.

He sat on a kind of chaise-longue, wicker and comfortable with cushions; and took an account-book out of the bag. There were columns of names, against each name a sum of money: two rupees, five rupees and so on. I don't think I bothered even to look at the name of the orphanage—I was too interested in this "inmate." I wrote my name in the book and gave him a ten-rupee note, which he carefully stowed in a pocket of the valise: if he were a confidence-trickster, he deserved to get away with it—the frankness in his eyes and the air of authority with which he handled his book and bag were so wonderfully convincing. "You give me smoke?" he said—his low, gentle voice was in the midst of breaking— and took a cigarette from a table beside him, adding, with a

29

quick, amused smile, "please?" It was the first time he had smiled. Then he lay back cosily, smoking, with his head weighing refreshingly into the cushions, the long, smooth immaculate throat stretched taut and his bare brown thighs and lolling calves languid along the settee. He was enjoying this tiny interlude of comfort, I could see; yet I felt there was some unidentified element of amusement in his enjoyment. He smoked in silence, his black eyes looking upwards, dreaming, at the fan; I sat watching his face.

He wasn't pretty in any key: from a casual glance one might even have called him plain. But, watching him, I found myself feeling a growing and warming pleasure: the kind of pleasure one may find in the rarities of an unknown flower that's both oddly beautiful and excitingly sensual; he was like some strange pale-brown orchid—a faintly Semitic orchid—whose petals and fronds and shadowed cavities seem both to ogle and entrance. There was sweetness and tenderness in his face, and an air of sadness that I interpreted as *need*; as well as a kind of pouting fleshiness about the mouth and nose which might be the mark of a voluptuary and which to my eye seemed to point to a northern India origin: I told myself he was a Moslem. But above all, there was about his face an indefinable distinction: it seemed to communicate a difference that was not only unique—for every face is unique —but that also meant some fascinating quality of mind or character. I found myself wanting to know what this quality was: I found myself thinking that this might be the sort of quality I should like to fall in love with.

He saw me watching him, and blew out a lungful of smoke. Then he asked brightly: "You like boyfuck?" This was a bit of dialogue that has stayed with me for the rest of time and kept its impact freshly ever since. Other conversational fragments have lingered on, more or less intact, from down the years; but these three words still sound in my mind, just as they were uttered. The ripening voice had kept some treble overtones: there was something like a shrill sob in its touching instability. He said "boyfuck" without the hyphen, As if it were a cheerful little word as common in his daily vocabulary as "football" or "teatime": and he might have been asking: "Do you like asparagus?" or, perhaps, proposing blind man's buff to amuse the children. But the bright light in his eyes told me that he wanted to be amused himself.

"Yes? You like boyfuck?" he repeated.

"It all depends," I said, "on what you mean by *fuck*"; and began to explain that I wasn't capable of buggery in either role. . . .

"What you like," he said, "I like"; and squashed out his cigarette in an ashtray. In a flash I was beside him, and half carried him over to the bed; the battered old hat fell off, and when he flopped down, the loose damp hair fanned over the white pillow like a wreath of black flame. I pulled his shirt over his head; for a moment he lay with his arms stretched back over the pillow, so that tiny beads of sweat showed in the tender hollows of his hairless armpits. I don't know why it is that certain parts of an adolescent boy's body seem so tender, so vulnerable and touching, so innocent, so much *in need* : the armpits, the nape of the neck, the hollows behind the knees, the heartrending narrowness across the shoulders. Why is this heartrending? Why should one be yearningly touched by the sight of these insusceptible and passionless corners of youthful flesh? I suppose it's because, within a frame and spirit that's growing and striving towards heftiness and heartiness and self-sufficiency, these seem cases of tender defenceless childishness that ask for love and protection : areas of innocence that appeal not to the fleshly sexual impulses but to the mothering and guardian-angel emotion which is or ought to be a part of every boy-lover's sexual personality.

He brought his knees up to his nose and had his pants off in a trice; there were no drawers underneath. Then he stretched his legs out, prone on his back, while his eyes watched me, a look of faint amusement dappling like flickered sunshine his puzzling expression. The beauty of his body, glabrous as parchment and now seeming the colour of dark honey, made me almost giddy : the lovely soft flatness of his belly, the tiny span of the hips, the moulded heaving arch of the fleshless ribs. I felt I had never seen skin so smooth and unblemished—hairless as marble except for the twin black whisps of fluff on either side of the groin.

And then I saw that he was not a Moslem : he wasn't circumcized.

I wondered about his age: Thirteen I guessed, or even twelve—yet he might be older. I asked him.

"Fifteen," he answered: "that's what they said at the orphanage." I could believe he was fifteen; especially when looking again at his face, I detected once more that elusive note of maturity behind the boyishness of his expression—although so young was he bodily that not a whorl of adolescent down appeared on his cheek. I thought of all the nonsense that's talked and written about the "early onset of puberty" in the Orient and other climatically benign regions of the earth: in a lifetime of observation I have found that in the Far and Middle East, in Africa and the Mediterranean, the beginning of adolescence comes about the same year as anywhere elese, even allowing for boys' frequent vagueness in those parts about their actual age—anywhere between twelve and fifteen. The proportion of precocities or of dilatory developments seemed to me about the same as I'd come across in European climes. And so, I reasoned, fifteen was probably this sweet brown creature's age; orphanages were sure to get facts like ages right, if nothing else.

"You don't want to take your clothes off?" he asked a trifle fretfully.

*　　　*　　　*

I can't remember the details of the next hour (or half-an-hour or three hours or whatever it was: a tiny aeon of timelessness which no clock could measure). There remains only an impression: the kind of impression left by a fevered night of exquisite half-dream: a misty and undulating impression of slippery warmth and softness, of wet tongues and lips abandoning their separable selves in the dazzling sweet darkness of fusion—the distinction of "my tongue," "your mouth," dissolved into the amalgam of "ours"; of effluvium and flavour, and the passionate adventure of exploration; of the sweet pungency on the tongue of moist armpits; the voluptuous pressure of bloodwarm thighs smothering the ears in a satin embrace (oh, the dribbling kisses in the most secret cavities of the flesh, the elixir of the saliva's drenching of a tuft of downy hair!); of hands seeking—caressing, stroking, fondling, searching: endlessly flowing and straying with infinite tenderness, with worship for the body caressed and fond-led and searched and for the boy-spirit within it; of the ecstasy of clasping and being clasped, soft belly merging into soft belly, the delicious tensities of erection defying distension : of wandering fingers spelling out in the glaring darkness of sensation the conformations of the adored bone and flesh— the ripple of the ribs, the tiny titillating nipples, the hidden warmths of the gorge between the buttocks; of a yearning to absorb and consume and assimilate; of the rapturous play of tongue and palate on which seems to the sensual imagination a volume of tumescence of priapic endowment and portent; of the ultimate supreme paroxysms, separate and secret yet shared in the concord of emotion; an impression of dementia and ecstatic flesh bathed in sweat, and spittle—and a happiness beyond the range of thought or fancy.

How ridiculous these things look when written down! How ridiculous and often disgusting the doing of them seems when considered dispassionately! Yet they're the common stuff of lovemaking : often of the regular lovemaking between male and female. How on earth, or in heaven, can such happiness be wicked?

*　　　*　　　*

Afterwards, we lay and talked. He was perfectly at ease, showing none of the sheepishness or shamefacedness that too often follows a coming. My head was turned towards him : I felt I couldn't look at him long enough. Here, unreasoning romanticism was telling me, is the perfect love; but reason kept repeating : It's impossible, it's impossible. . . .

He spoke a serviceable orphanage-English; and I tried to lead him to talk about himself. But he was quickly worrying about the lateness of the afternoon : he had calls to make with his collecting book, he had to be back at the orphanage; he had time only for one question, and he kept harking back to it : "You take me with you?" was the theme. "Yes—*yes*? You take me to Kashmir, to Burma, to Japan to England?" (Oh God! How often have I heard this heartbreaking plea?) He would come to see me tomorrow, he said, at the same time; and I stretched over and stroked his sable head—I was dumb with happiness : I knew I couldn't take him with me, but I swore to myself then that somehow I should look after him—that by some miracle we should find a solution. We should talk it all over tomorrow; that evening I had to leave.

While he was dressing he began telling me about the massacres of recent weeks: how the streets were red with blood and strewn with the dead bodies of Hindus and Sikhs —there wasn't a Sikh left in Lahore, he said, now that all who hadn't been murdered had escaped across the new frontier to Amritsar in India. Except, he added, a few Sikhs who were in hiding, in disguise. And suddenly he stopped in the middle of doing up a sandal, and looked at me.

"I Sikh," he said. "I too Sikh."

"*You* a Sikh? But how can you be—where's your long hair and your iron bangle? What about those special drawers the Sikis wear?"

He had cut off his hair, he said; he'd buried the ritual bangle and dagger and drawers; he was in disguise. . . . He stood up, ready to go, the exercise-book and doctor's bag under his thin arm; he gave me no time to say anything more. I fumbled with money: "No, no," he said, "they find it maybe, they say I stolen. . . . Tomorrow, or next day when you take me away. . . ."

I could hear the bearers and cleaners starting on their evening business, the sound of water and the clanking of tin baths. It was late. "I go," he said, and looked at me once more: behind the flicker of sadness in the smile there seemed to me too (perhaps I was imagining things) an anxiety and a *need*. . . .

He was out on the sunbaked gravel—against its dusty yellow glare the olive-honey of his calves turned dark. He looked back once over his shoulder and said softly: "Tomorrow, tomorrow. . . ." As he walked away the tail of his shirt drooped absurdly over his tiny rump.

*   *   *

Common sense, and the fact that life in the city was almost back to normal, told me there was scarcely the smallest risk: the slaughter was over, the blood was dry. Pakistan had "won": the Moslems had killed as many Hindus as they had been able and had exterminated the people they hated most, the Sikhs. Surely a boy, looking little different from hundreds of Moslem boys, and with nothing—in his shirt and shorts—to mark him as non-Moslem, couldn't be in danger? Even if the killing were still going on, which is wasn't, nobody could notice this small anonymous creature. . . . *And yet he was a Sikh.* . . . That was the dreadful fact that kept intruding into common sense's comfortable argument. But there was nothing I could do to help settle it, beyond turning to the whisky bottle I wisely had brought to my room, and longing for tomorrow to come.

Next morning I had work: government people to see, calls to make, a cable to send. But I worked skin-deep: instead of politics and the latest news I could think only of Sikhs—of one small Sikh whose stainless tender body and sweet, puzzling face filled my mind. When I looked at the bland, wary expressions of the bureaucrats or shook the plump and expository hands of the politicians, I saw instead the boy's face and it was his satin skin that my fingers seemed to touch. The people I saw in the streets were blank figures, behind each of which I expected to find that slim small form in the skimpy shirt and shorts. I felt I was being carried through the morning in a bubble of rather agreeable fever from which, like vaguely seeing something blurred against the sun, I watched myself going through the motions of my work.

Dust-brown, brick-red, mustard-yellow: these are the colours I remember today from that morning of long ago; Lahore was an agglomerate of various tones of burnt sienna, garnished with blobs of the abrupt and irrelevantly over-bright greens of municipally watered foliage. The city was like an encampment lying at ease; one might have thought it asleep, if one forgot the pattering, babbling crowds milling through the dust. How could one believe that last week it had been a city of ferocious genocidal carnage? There lay over it the golden calm of a life that never changes: after the nightmare of slaughter, men, women and children had simply picked up what they'd dropped when it began. Catastrophe, where life is, human or not, seems generally to be followed by an astonishing and almost irrelevant resuscitation of the spirit: a beetle batted violently off the edge of a thirty-foot wall will lie dazed below for a moment and then, as if nothing had happened to it, resume its ordinary business on a brand new plane. People were going about their daily affairs as if they had never seen hot running human blood muddying this peaceful dust; Moslems and Hindus brushed by each other without a hint of difference.

But there were no Sikhs. The two or three said to have been left alive in the city after the great massacre and flight were hidden and disguised. But supposing, I kept thinking— oh God, supposing!—some rabid, fanatic Moslem, some madman whose eyes were still shot with hatred and the love of blood, were to recognize the boy as a Sikh : just one crazy killer was enough, like that famous single careless finger on the nuclear trigger. . . . And suddenly it occurred to me that I was calling the boy all the time in my mind "the boy" : I'd been so engrossed in him yesterday that I hadn't thought to ask his name.

At lunch in the gloomily grandiose hotel dining-room, try- ing to read the London newspapers, I found myself thinking about the orphanage. Again I'd been a bloody fool : I hadn't found out where the place was or what it was called; there were probably several orphanages here—a city of more than three-quarters of a million. All I had learned about it was that it sent its orphans out begging for funds from British visitors, from official Christians, that is : it was, presumably, a Chris- tian orphanage, run by (I was guessing) some Protestant missionaries—probably Methodists; an orphanage which, again presumably, picked up most of its orphans at birth or soon after and hurriedly Methodized them. It seemed odd, I thought, for a Sikh orphan to be in the place; and odder, if he'd been christianized, that he should so recently have been wearing Sikh emblems. His face, which by now was obsessing me, looked back at me from the gilt-framed mirrors on the walls : pale as wild honey, full-lipped and promising fleshiness later, features faintly Semitic. It was the face of a Sikh; which meant the face of a Punjabi—a face indeed that might have been bred anywhere along Alexander's route from Persia eastwards into India. . . . But christianized, surely, he *wouldn't* have been wearing those Sikh emblems. . . .? And was his name followed by the honorific "Singh" common to all men of his sect? I hadn't even *asked* his name. . . .

And suddenly I saw daylight : in a flash I was certain of one thing—the obviousness of it came to me with such a rush that I involuntarily gave a great sweep with the newspaper I was supposed to be reading, and swept the electroplated currydish on to the floor with a fearful clatter. I remember how the sedate men at the other tables turned to stare at me and then, being well-bred or wanting to seem well-bred, quickly looked away; I remember how horrid the curry looked lying on the "oriental" tiling. And I remember the look of obsequious disdain on the dark face of the "bearer," as grand in dress and bearing as a maharajah, before signalling for the subservient, shuffling "sweepers" to come and clear up the mess.

Of course: the boy wasn't a Sikh at all. He couldn't be: were he a Sikh, he wouldn't have been brought up where he was. The Sikhs, rich and powerful and clannish wherever they were, from Hong Kong to Aden and the east African coast but especially in their homeland of the Punjab, would never allow one of their offspring, whatever its circumstances, to be gathered up by Christian charity; as a community, they've money to burn, and would have their own institutions for their own young, supported by their own funds, inspired by their own pride. The shaggy Sikhs, whose manes, beards and bodily hair must be allowed to grow from childhood unclipped, are, like Samson, historically famed for strength and military valour; another birthright conferred by the Sikh faith is, oddly, a remarkable aptitude for money-making: the bulky forms of Sikh watchmen in Singapore and elsewhere, reclining on their trestle-beds on the shaded pavements and adding up their money-lending profits, fatten on weekly interest—and, enough capital garnered, they go on to become building contractors. Once in New Delhi I was given tea by five millionaires: all Sikhs, all contractors, and all British knights. These were the thoughts that brought me to the obvious: No, the Sikhs weren't the people to leave their orphans to subsist on door-to-door collections from Christians. The boy could *not* be a Sikh. . . .

* * *

There was an hour to go before his coming: an hour of impatience to be looking once more at that body of old ivory, to be touching again that sentient skin, to be loving instantly and for ever that face and flesh. Killing the hour I set about trying to work out this new perplexity—the enigma of a boy's mind who gives himself out to be a Sikh just when every

37

Sikh in sight has been slaughtered, when everything the eye falls on seems tinged with the colour of Sikh blood. What role he secretly played in this crazy fantasy I couldn't guess: a heroical one perhaps—or did he in some murky emotional way, see himself in the sacrificial part of victim? I suppose the psychologists would find one of those hideous and pretentious words of theirs for it: I could only add this latest puzzle to those tiny symptoms which, scarcely heeded in yesterday's excitement, now seemed dark with meaning: his grown-up self-composure, almost brashness perhaps; the overglib *naïveté* (or was it canniness?) of his "You like boyfuck?"; the strange lines of maturity that elusively seemed to play over his almost quizzical boy's face; the plea or the uncertainty that I thought I could read in those yellow-black half-wild eyes: I told myself it all pointed to some *lack,* some need in the boy's heart and mind, which no institution like an orphanage—even if it gave him all the physical food he could eat—could fill but which I, perhaps, could. . . . a lack, surely, of affection and gentleness and something like *mothering* . . . things that I could try to give—things that I swore then I would try to give. . . .

The creeping seconds took an hour to make a minute; I opened the shutters and even a distant footstep had me running to the window. I couldn't read or even sit; I walked up and down and absurdly tidied up, by taking things from where they belonged and putting them elsewhere. I tried to think out a practical plan, a way of arranging for him to join me: but rational thinking refused to work properly— its pieces kept scattering behind the image of a honey-brown body. . . . The waiting was becoming unbearable; when my watch showed that he should be here I went out into the glare of the gravel drive and *willed* him to turn through the gate from the main road. We most of us believe that if we look far enough for the longed-for person, the person will come; it's a bit of sympathetic magic, I suppose: if I go out to meet the beloved, won't the beloved come to meet me . . .?

*   *   *

This story has a beginning; perhaps a middle. It has no end. Today, twenty years later, it still has no end: I have only done twenty years of my life sentence.

The boy didn't come. Early that evening I had to leave for Calcutta, and from there fly on to Burma. I never saw him again; I never learned who or what he was. For twenty years it's been as if I'd never seen him—or seen him no more substantially than in some Elysian daydream; yet almost daily since that afternoon in Lahore, every incident of it has been reenacted: sometimes in the waking imagination, sometimes in the vivid lunacy of nightmare. And I've never ceased to feel the guilt of my betrayal: true I promised nothing to him out loud, but I'd sworn to myself silently on his behalf. And all that time I have been harassed and nagged by one question: Why didn't he come? Was it simply because he forgot, or couldn't be bothered? Was it because he got into trouble with the orphanage authorities—those ogres of both sexes who run such places? Or was it because he was, after all, really a Sikh...?

*　　*　　*

At the time, once it was clear he wasn't coming, I knew there was nothing I could do: I knew that the worldly net which catches us poor fish was, as usual, too strong for us—and the higher one gets from the bottom of the net, the closer the mesh becomes. There was no escaping it. The people who employed me had spent a lot of money to get me where I was and where I was going; I owed them work against a deadline, and had already been paid for a good deal of it. I *had* to go. So there were two hours left in which to find a small brown boy whose name I didn't know, whose address I didn't know: whose age, whereabouts, religion, caste, race, parentage, origins and history I didn't know; and this in a country where census records and *état civil* registers were scant. I knew I could do nothing; I left Lahore, on time; and the boy, for ever.

Afterwards, when it was too late and the practical dilemma was behind me; when, free of the distracting imbroglio of hard facts, I could look at the moral or idealist conundrum from the side; when, no longer caught in that particular net of social reality, I hadn't got to make a decision—then, of course, I saw I'd been a heel: mean and treacherous or contemptibly gutless; I saw that I should have made a bonfire of all those staid pieces of comfortable furniture like common

39

sense and practicality and regard for duty—I should have thrown everything up and set about looking after the boy. But what good could I have been to him without the means of looking after him, without an income? It's not often one can break out of the social net without hanging oneself in the mesh.

To every lover of boys comes this dilemma at least once in his life: the harrowing, heart-quickening appeal: "You take me with you?"

TEL AVIV

WHAT AN exquisite sampler of the world's boyhood Israel was! I say "was," because I'm writing of a summer exactly twenty years ago: when Israel the full-fledged sovereign State, only two or three months out of the nest, was fighting her first war against the Arab armies, and winning her first victory over them. Even then one was struck by the physical appearance of the young "sabras," the boys born on this soil of Zion—whose fathers and grandfathers too had often been born here—and reared to the open air and outdoor work on the land: Israel was already breeding a new race of what one might call Hebrew un-Jews: a breed of neo-Jews who, reacting biologically to the novel environment into which they were being born and to the different values and attitudes to which they were being bred, were discarding the characteristics, physical as well as moral, that had labelled their forefathers for thousands of years. This new race of un-Jews was growing up snub-nosed, fair-haired and blue-eyed; these neo-Jewish sabras were arrogantly proud of the nationhood they were building and the Hebrew they were speaking, but they neither resembled in feature, nor saw themselves reflected in, the old traditional Jewry they now only heard about like something out of history. But this was twenty years ago; today those sabra boys I knew and saw are between thirty and forty years old, and many of them the fathers of families: the sabras now must number tens of thousands and form the robust home-bred neo-Jewish core of the Israeli nation.

Already in those days, around the almost Nordic types of the sabra boys, one saw nearly every style the human mould was capable of producing—from the Spanish and

Portuguese good looks of the Sephardis, through the ringleted puritans from the Rumanian ghettos and the "Arab" Jews of North Africa, to the beautiful Yemenites whose skins were as immaculately black as the Tamils of southern India. Missing only were Negro Africans and types from the Extreme Orient. Are there no Jews of Black African descent —no Jews from China, Japan or at least the Philippines? It seems a pity that the racial spectrum of Israel should be incomplete : what a perfect multiracial State the world could have here, embracing all the peoples of every kind and colour, united only by that mysterious quality and awareness, para-doxically both eclectic and exclusive, which we know as Jewishness. . . .

This delightfully variegated spectrum, though incomplete, could be seen most attractively and revealingly, I found, through the prism of the bathing place which spread then along the beach below the old Kaethe Dan Hotel—a hotel which, so excellent in those days, no longer exists, I have to my regret been told; though a new and grander "Dan Hotel" has arisen in another spot. There was a narrow lane, I seem to remember, which took one to the rear of the Kaethe Dan, and then, by a flight of stone steps, one ran down to the vast, glittering expanse of the Phoenician shore. On this stretch of the beach, a mile or two north of Jaffa and near the point where that famous arms-smuggling ship was wrecked in British days, with the backs of the new villadom of Tel Aviv looking down on them from embankment-height with averted suburban eyes, stood the old-fashioned wooden installations of the municipal "lido"—dressing-rooms, showers, and so on; all raised on lofty stilts above any onslaught from the sea, though the water here was so shallow and the Mediterranean tide so minutely varying that there didn't seem much danger. But to the boys who bathed there day after day through the long hot summer of 1948 these stilts, and the convenient height to which they raised the wooden flooring of the showers and dressing-rooms, were of the utmost importance : they allowed plenty of head-room for prowling or standing beneath the boards and peering up through the cracks between the planks. Water raining from the floor of any one segment of the women's showers, showed that that compartment was being used. . . .

There were private cabins for families or men who wanted one; but the boys, and myself always, used a great barrack of a dressing-room—it cost almost nothing to undress there and hang one's clothes on a peg: I never heard of any thieving while people were out on the sands, and certainly never experienced any myself.

After school in the afternoons, and all the morning during holidays, this vast changing-room—like a Malay longhouse, a visitor from those parts would say—was thronged with a wonderful assortment of naked boys' bodies: boys pulling off their shirts and pants and stretching for a moment in the joyous exemption given by nudity before stepping into their swimming trunks; boys wet from the sea with drops still quivering on their skins like dew, and others with a sopping forelock dripping into their eyes; boys towelling at their backs and shoulders as if manning a two-handed saw; boys sitting back naked on a bench, in an ecstasy of physical relaxation after the exertions of a long swim; boys sitting naked on a bench absorbedly fingering and eyeing their own genitals; boys exhibiting to each other the evidence of their approach to adulthood. . . . Dark-skinned boys with beautiful Arab faces; pug-nosed sabras with creamy skins and eyes the colour of the sky; the varying types of every branch of European Jewry; boys of all shades of colour and all stages of blossoming growth: an enthralling conspectus of circumcized boyhood. . . .

The sabras, and immigrant boys at the higher schools, spoke Hebrew, modernized as far as possible to fit the technological age: it was the language of the new Israeli élite; others spoke Yiddish, the *lingua franca* of Europe; and yet others the Jewish-Arabic dialect of their land of birth. I could rarely understand their conversation—and there was always the same sweet cacophony of shouting that a crowd of gabbling boys creates anywhere in the world. But sometimes I could get their meaning: I recall one afternoon when a lanky, lonely boy of about sixteen, drying himself with a leisurely, aloof sort of luxury, suddenly, and apparently without the slightest awareness, became dowered with an erection of such magnitude and aggressiveness as one wouldn't have guessed possible, looking at him a couple of minutes earlier. He continued calmly to towel himself in a fastidious and

43

luxuriating way, apparently perfectly unmindful of the enormous phallus he was displaying; while the huge organ itself, too rigid to be said to swing or sway, canted back and forth in accord with the delicate writhings of his arms and shoulders like a magnificent figurehead at the prow of a gently rolling ship. As soon as this was noticed by the other boys, it brought hoots of jeering and pretended horror and mock-modest vilification, but mostly of course, jeers and sarcastic obscenities—as I could tell from the crowd of scoffing faces and from my own familiarity with the behaviour of boys. But the owner of the subject of all this uproar wasn't in the least put out; he went on dabbing his damp hair with his towel and gazed at his yelling tormentors with serene disdain, while his immense penis, still flushed and proudly upstanding, seemed to regard them with similar scorn. And then, in what I took to be elegant Hebrew, he silenced them all with an authority and clarity which I had no difficulty in interpreting: "First of all what's happened to me is perfectly natural and happens to all of you, as you know; secondly, if I get the horn it's no business of yours just as it's none of mine if you get it; and thirdly, if my cock stands up, it's not the sight of any of you that makes it do so!" Anyway, the jeers and the shouting instantly stopped after his unruffled little speech, and without another glance at the others he leisurely began to put on his clothes.

Outside on the sands, the scene was that of any family seaside resort—except beneath the women's showers and dressing-rooms, where behaviour among the shadows between the concrete pillars which supported them must have seemed peculiar to anybody who didn't understand what was going on. Plump matrons, innocently unembarrassed by the volumes of flesh which seemed to spill over the confines of their swimsuits, sat like comfortable hens in the soft sand and nagged, clucking, at their infant families; charming children of all sorts dug with spades or played ball or ran dripping back from the sea to their mothers; middle-aged men, lean and fat, with dignified professorial faces, reclined beneath large sunshades and read volumes in German or Hebrew; dark-haired girls with crimson mouths and waggling breasts and buttocks tripped back and forth self-consciously wearing the latest beach-fashions to arrive from Europe. And all the while, with nobody visibly paying any attention, the most extraordinary semblance of a ballet was being danced by an all-male cast under the women's quarters—and especially beneath the flooring of the showers, from which a constant rain of water sprayed over the dancers and into the eyes of their upturned faces. A varying number of boys and young men—in age everything from twelve to twenty or even more —would all day be prancing and pirouetting, like entranced dervishes or a set of marionettes, over the rectangles of shadowed sand, uncannily chill and damp, from which the sun was for ever held off by the buildings above. These bands of agitated boys, made oblivious by their passionate absorption of everybody around them, performed a kind of cakewalk sideways, forwards and backwards: their knees bent, their spines curved rearwards almost to the point of overtoppling, and their heads tilted back upon their shoulders, their eyes starting from their sockets in the effort to discern *something* through what gaps could be found between the planking above their noses. Since all of them were wearing nothing but a clinging pair of trunks, it was for anybody to see when the emotional reaction of one of these eager young voyeurs to what he saw, or hoped to see, became physically manifest. . . . I have only once again, and in one other place, come across a similar display of public scopophilia; this was many years later, in Sicily, and I was instantly reminded of those curious, and rather exhilarating, scenes on the Tel Aviv shore. At Messina there took place every summer an important trade fair for which various buildings and installations were specially erected. Among these was a spacious platform or stage of wooden planks which, supported by an intricate scaffolding of steel tubing, jutted out to the sea's edge and over a narrow foreshore of rocks in whose crannies the boys left their clothes while they bathed—this was ordinarily an empty and rather scruffy part of Messina's northern extremity. But once the fair was underway, and the public was walking about this wooden platform, the boys would always be clambering over the scaffolding, hanging on with their toes like parrots, and peering up through the boards to see what they could see—at best, I suppose, a fleeting peep at a female knicker, and to get that would require a lot of luck.

At Tel Aviv, I thought as I watched these frustrated Sicilian boys, there was at any rate a chance of real nudity. . . .

One morning, on that beach, I saw a boy—about fourteen he looked—sitting in a kind of bowl he'd scooped out of the sand, with his back against one of the concrete stilts and his legs stretched out in front of him—he was engrossed in the task of ploughing out with his heels a second cavity so that a kind of saddle was forming under his knees. I knew exactly what he was feeling; the warm, comfortable, relaxing rest-fulness of that hump of sand in the hollow of his knees—like throwing one's legs over the arm of a sofa : this was just what I always found myself doing when daydreaming in the sand. He wore a dirty-white pair of running pants; a couple of ragged garments, rolled into a bundle, were beside him. His hair was very dark, above an almost ivory-white skin—the sort that only goes sallow with the sun; his charmingly undistinguished face, snubby and very boy-like, seemed to me vaguely central European—Polish, perhaps. He had dark grey-green eyes; if there were anything Semitic about his face, it was a faint fleshiness of the lips—a thick red mouth, it was : an exotic, even oriental, mouth. He was looking very solemn, frowning over the ploughing of his heels.

I thought he might speak Yiddish, which my German would let me mostly understand; but when I got talking to him I found he was a sabra and knew, besides a basic Hebrew (it can't have been more than basic), a kind of "menial English"—the English of messenger-boys and street-hawkers picked up in his fourteen years under British tute-lage. So once we got started our conversation flowed. But my first approach was gingerly, not knowing what our conversa-tional resources were : I simply sat down beside him as if that was just where I'd naturally want to sit, and held out my cigarettes under his nose as if that was what I always did wherever I was. This jerked him out of his mooning, and in the second of surprise his green eyes seemed to expand all round like Japanese paper lilies in water; then he gave me a sidelong pout of cautious evaluation which quickly turned into a doubtful half-grin—but he took a cigarette and leaned across for me to give him a light from mine.

His name was Shlomo, which delighted me : I always want charming boys to have charming names. I can't say he showed signs, while I knew him, of acquiring anything like the wisdom of his namesake, Solomon; but neither did he do anything downright silly. He'd been in Tel Aviv all his life and his parents, so far as I could understand, had come from some region of the Austro-Hungarian border—he wasn't sure himself what country his family's had been. He was born in Palestine; now he was Israeli—that was good enough for him.

By this time I'd left the hotel and had found a room in a private house—the room had its own entrance and an old-fashioned tin bath which one filled with a can. I wrote down the address for him and told Shlomo that if he called there I might have a job for him—emptying the bath and so on, I indicated. Then I had to be off. "S'long," he said; and I didn't expect to see him again. But that evening, just as I was filling the can for my bath, he appeared; and when I had to go out and he left for his home, he said: "S'long"—a kind of cross between "so long" and the Israeli hail-or-farewell *shalom*. It was his favourite bit of English: every time he went out of the room, he said "S'long," and always when he set off at the end of a day.

We got on very well. He was slow and stolid but always genuine. Behind those enticing lips there was no warmth; in his little dutiful heart there was absolute loyalty but little affection: he was like a gentle dog that's touchingly faithful to the hand that feeds it. For nearly two months he was my Argus—Argus as a puppy: devoted and unfailing: he seemed to have no desires more lofty or interesting than sweeping out my room and fetching water for the bath.

And then a cable came, ordering me to move to some other country at once. I came back to my room and found him waiting there, with the bath all laid out and the water heating. "Shlomo," I said, "I've got to go away at once. Here are all the wages I owe you, and here's this much more besides, as a present. Dear Shlomo, now we've got to say goodbye—"

"S'long," he said: gave a casual wave, and was gone. . . .

RANGOON

EACH TIME I come upon a stretch of shining water, and boys
bathing in it, and the colour of their flesh glowing and paling
and gilding under the play of the sun, I see too, as if behind
a cloud that always in my mind hangs sombrely in the sky,
the memory of another picture : the same sunlight plays, no
less lightly and brightly, no less warmly, upon a small naked,
dangling body being carried up into the town from the
Rangoon waterfront—legs hanging limp down a man's chest,
ebony round head bobbing behind the man's back, and the
tiny tender buttocks arched over his shoulder; while a straggle
of silent boys follow, silent with awe or fear or the need to
gape, some of them naked and still dripping from the river.

Where hundreds of boys bathe, and dozens of them can
hardly swim, the thing to marvel at is the small number who
even get into difficulties and have to be fished out by their
friends; one may also marvel at the number of people who,
the newspapers report, get drowned at those well-regulated
bathing resorts and pools where the public is protected by
lifeguards, danger flags, safety zones, and printed notices
telling the customers what they mustn't do. But such com-
parisons aren't much comfort when one's among a mob of
solemn-eyed Burmese boys, behind a heart-breaking small
dangling corpse. . . .

All my life I've needed the propinquity of water; as a dog
needs the nearness of open land I like to live on the water's
edge, and to hear the waves; or on small islands, so as to be
closely surrounded by the sea; if I've had to live inland, away
from a shore, I've always felt uneasy and bereft, unless at
least a lake or an adequate river were within handy reach.

And all my life, given sunshine and warmth, I've been happiest when bathing and basking : for the sake, partly, of the sensuous luxuries of sun and water, and partly—who would want to deny it?—for the sake of those sexual appurtenances of bathing which, to him who is susceptible to them, are the chief of its charms : the delicious emotions which youthful and artless nudity inevitably give one—the blissful pleasure of contemplating naked boys.

And so, when I came to Rangoon, I made for the waterfront : those sandy-brown quays, sparkling like gold dust, above the smoky port where the big ships lay, against which were jammed a kaleidoscopic huddle of small river and coastal craft that had brought a mixed bag of cargoes from all round the seaboard of the Bay of Bengal—birds' nests from the Siamese coast for Chinese soup, printed cottons from Calcutta, tin, perhaps, from Penang, modish shoes from Hong Kong or Singapore.

On the day I met Maung Tay Ba the burning blue of the sky seemed filtered by a thin haze, as if a lightly smoked film had been laid over it; a halo of dark vapour hung over the docks down-river where the steamers lay : among them a couple of ships of the British India line, with their sheer black hulls and black funnels—so familiar (and even familial) to generations of "Anglo-Indians"—soldiers, civil servants, tea-planters—journeying outwardbound to some station in India or going "home" for a few months' leave.

A string of native vessels lay moored alongside : small sailing sampans and a variety of craft converted from sail to power—and abreast of them a second line of boats lay, and beyond that a third : so that the boys could jump from deck to deck and dive into the brown stream of the Rangoon River from the bulwarks of the outermost craft. There were dozens of the boys—there seemed hundreds : darting and dancing and diving, laughing and shouting, dripping and glistening in the glassy light : they came and went, crossed and mingled and recrossed, golden and gleaming, light-limbed and bright-eyed, in a constant kind of choreographic scramble : lords, each one of them at that moment, of the world in the gorgeous freedom of their nudity.

Suddenly, where I sat on a quayside bollard, I found myself looking into two of the blackest eyes I'd ever seen, and a gay little grinning yellow face—it was more a smile than a grin—which had popped up at my feet, with cascading wet hair like spouts of black water, from between the quay and the wooden planks of a barge. He climbed up ashore, still grinning, stood for a moment lemon-coloured in the sunlight, quite naked, shook the wet off with a flutter of his arms like a bird in a bath, and took a running header over the bows of the barge. I had time to have engraved on my mind the image of a featherweight boy's body, yet compact and proportioned like the scale-model of a mature man.

It wouldn't be true to say that I thought no more about him—I thought a great deal about him, as one does about anything one's seen that's seemed startlingly out of the ordinary, anything of unusual beauty or unusually arousing. But I didn't expect to see him again, among the seething and dazzlingly chromatic myriads that thronged the Rangoon streets. I thought of the sweet nature that was plainly visible behind the impishness of the grin; of the firm, flawless, moulded texture of that yellow flesh. I thought of the surprising maturity of the figure, and yet the absolute boyishness of it; and of the shining black pools of those eyes, in whose lucent deepness seemed to lie waiting such funds of young emotion —of affection, perhaps, of fiery desire or ambition, of loneliness or need. And I thought of that body : of the sexual ripeness that it touchingly displayed. And, as I walked back to the Strand Hotel through the heat and the spicy air, my imagination played with the absurd notion of having that yellow-tinted youth as a companion during the month or so I was going to stay in Burma—did any of those old kings in classical Mandalay possess an attendant half so delightful? Absurd, of course, the notion was; and when, in the hotel room, commodiously neuter like any hotel room, I settled down to do some work, I put it right out of my mind and tucked the boy's image away somewhere out of thought.

And almost at once, when I next turned out of the hotel door, I met him again. I don't know if he had come there on purpose, guessing that the Englishman he had seen on the quayside (who was bound to be rich) would be staying at the Strand Hotel. Probably yes : yet I didn't find him obviously stationed outside the hotel entrance; he was a little way along the river embankment—and how could he know I wouldn't be walking in the opposite direction? And if he had stationed himself there on purpose—well, why not? On what moral grounds, for God's sake, could the most virtuous prissy prig reprove him? "They hang around, these native boys, just to see what they can get—and one wouldn't like to think what they're willing to do!" That's the kind of remark the English visitors used to make when they had colonies to visit. Well, why shouldn't they hang around to see what they can get? Isn't that what most people are doing anyway most of their lives? To see what they can get: sexual, or financial, or snob-social—one of the three.

He was sitting on his heels by the pavement edge, with his sarong tucked up from behind between his hams and his calves and in front pulled down over his knees; he was doodling in the dust with a piece of stick. He wore nothing except the sarong: bare-footed and bare-bodied down to the waist: his tiny nipples were like pepper-corns poised on the golden pallor of his breast. When he saw me he gave the same smiling grin as before: a smile of *sharing,* as if there were something we both understood— it was a smile of recognition, containing neither surprise nor expectancy: his look expected nothing. Then he turned his head down again to the road, and went on drawing in the dust.

"D'you want a cigarette?" I asked, holding out a packet almost against his nose, so that he should be in no doubt, supposing he knew no English, what I was up to. He helped himself, delicately, at once; with the same frank smile—it seemed to say that though he wasn't asking for a cigarette, it was understood between us that one was his if he wanted it.

"You got light?" he said. His voice was a low-pitched contralto, dulcet as a dove's.

And then—after, I suppose, some exchange of proposal and consent that I can't now recall—he was walking along beside me, his bare leather-coloured feet moving silently and insensibly, like a dog's pads: his toes were stubby with broad squat nails, and the skin of his feet, browned by lifelong bareness, was rough and crumbled like a tortoise's hide. He walked lightly, and yet with a springing athlete's stride, with none of that adolescent giving at the knees and with his square young shoulders held back; he walked with the air of a patrician—I felt at first that to turn and look at his face would be an impertinence, like staring.

As we went along—vaguely along the river "strand," as that thoroughfare was called, for I had not thought of where to go or what to do—I tried, gently, to ask him questions about himself. I knew no Burmese, and he, I found, had scarcely any English; yet as one always can, all the world over, when concord is mutually felt, we got most of each other's meaning. And now, since three-quarters of our language was lip-language, and eye-language, and the eloquence of mouth and head and hands, I had to look at him—at the sweet and artless candour of that smile, and the confidence that I thought I could discern beneath the sparkling black surface of the eyes; and at the full scarlet luxury of his lips. His face was pleasantly oval; his small nose the impeccable shape that's the privilege of most Burmese : his real distinction lay not in his features but in the expression of them—their dancing mobility like light on water, and the human warmth of his smile and eyes. His age, I guessed, could be anything from twelve to fifteen—his emotional desires, probably, no more complicated than a child's.

He wasn't, as I'd first thought, a waif : he had a home somewhere among the teeming tenements of Rangoon, and he had a mother with some younger children; she kept the family going by doing laundry for some British firm's employees. There wasn't a father : he'd disappeared, it seemed, some time during the social and political turmoils between the end of the war against the Japanese and the revolution against the British.

He told me his name was Maung Tay Ba, and that's what I henceforward called him; for I never mastered Burmese nicknames or diminutives, and never discovered what he was called at home or by his friends. *Maung* is a common honorific—something in the way of the Burmese "mister"; and is more general, I think, than *U* or *Thakin*—this last is perhaps a monkish term. So Maung Tay Ba he remained for me : a bit of a mouthful when murmured as the hub of encircling endearments.

His sarong—which in Burma is called a *loonghi*, the *g* hard as in *"ghee"*—was very clean and almost diaphanous as if his mother washed it very often; its thin cotton was printed in a tartan-like crisscross of green and pale yellow —tints of a lemon-tree's foliage for the embellishment of his own lemon-skin! But it was threadbare and frayed, and he was growing out of it—its hem was well above his ankles.

"What would you like me to buy you?" I asked, or rather mimed: I couldn't think of any other conversational opening.

"Shirt," he answered, "English shirt." He gave me again that frank, understanding smile that seemed to confer a perfect equality of partnership in the notion of this shirt: I would buy it, he would wear it—it would be our shirt. At the same time he illustrated the shirt with his hands over his shoulders and breast, and down his loins—it was plainly to be the style of shirt then still prevailing with a tail, which I supposed would hang outside his loonghi in the way of the Indian mode.

"Isn't there anything else?" I went on. "A new sarong— a new loonghi? And some sandals? Wouldn't your feet be happier in sandals?" I made him understand by seizing a fold of his garment, and pointing to my own sandals and to his feet.

He understood. His enchanting mouth curved into a shy, deprecating pout of imprimatur—as much as to say, Well, if you want to, it's up to you—I'm not asking for it.

I gave him some money and told him to bring what he bought to my room at the Strand Hotel. "I only hope they let you up," I added; but I didn't think he understood: his smile as he moved away seemed to fill all his face and eyes. Then he walked swiftly away, with the quick springing steps of a runner.

*   *   *

At the hotel I told the "desk" that a messenger-boy would be bringing some parcels: would they send him up at once? In those days, although Burma was already an independent and sovereign State, a white man at a hotel like the Strand was still the symbol of the "raj"—of, that is, the most influential and profitable sort of visitor; yet this wasn't the chief reason for the permissive attitudes of such places: in the Far East generally, and in the countries of South-East Asia especially, there never was, and let's hope there never will be, either the dirty-mindedness or the puritanism of the "progressive" West. If a half-naked adolescent of the lowest class went up to a visitor's room, the hotel staff didn't *think* about it or anything of it; their minds didn't start working along prying and prurient ways; or if some sexual whisper did enter into their meditation, they'd dismiss is as being no business of theirs.

So when Maung Tay Ba did present himself to the hall porter he was immediately given directions about finding my number, and sent straight up. With pleasure and timidity mingling in his smile, he displayed his purchases over the bed, and held out a fistful of coins : he must have bought the things in the cheapest bazaar he could find—I'd expected a third of the small change he brought. But he wouldn't put on any of his new things; he said he was dirty, first he must wash. Then he walked quickly over to the shower which, with the w.c., occupied a tiled alcove in a corner of the room, and pushed aside the splash curtain. "Good," he said, laughing with approval, "English bath very good. Me bath?" Without waiting for a Yes or No, he loosened the tucked-in fold that held his loonghi round his waist, dropped it to the floor, and stepped out of it as bare as an Asian Eros.

Before I joined him beneath the shower, I stood back and watched him : the lemon-gold convolutions of his flexuous body, the pearly runnels of shower-water, cloudy with soap, spilling down his skin like rain on lemon-peel. I thought I'd never seen such a perfectly constructed model of a grown man : shoulders squared for his height as a mature athlete's; the neatly ribbed torso converging like the sides of a wedge to waist and hips as fine as a bush-buck's. The chest was wide and full and yet still a boy's; his frame had none of the gangling puniness of an adolescent's but all its lightness and grace. I couldn't remember ever seeing before a body that seemed so purely beautiful : he was like Michelangelo's David in miniature. Later, I was often to see him in that figure's loose and casual stance of absolute physical assurance. When he had dried he walked over to the bed and lay down, as if this were a matter of course.

"Now we do playing?" he asked, with that same candid smile. "You like, please?"

His erotic expectations were humble, I found—nothing beyond his small, boyish experience. He enjoyed the warmth and softness and affection of hugging—especially, I think, the affection; but kissing he refused, turning away his face with a little shy laugh; and all he wanted after that was a quick and high-spirited masturbation, as if it were something of a joke or a game—content at first to do it himself, but interested and apparently pleased when I did it for him. And that was the totality of sex for him—it was what one might call small-boys'-sex; and he shrank from any sign of a move to go beyond it. And I, of course, was perfectly happy to leave it at that: whatever pleased him was good enough for me—he was such a delightful and decorative companion: to look at him alone was a joy that didn't seem to dwindle and the beaming honesty of his smile was like a pick-me-up. But it was the plea in his eyes and smile that made him so precious: a plea for affection, for fondness—a plea that within a day had become the thing it pled for: affection itself. In the gaiety and compassion and truth of his expression I could soon read that combination of tenderness and liking and trust that means absolute friendship. That's what I quickly discovered: what he wanted, needed, wasn't the kind of capricious, exacting, love which is sexual passion but the calm, gentle, trustworthy love that's affection; and this to me was far more important—and I had that gentle boyish friendship with me day and night, like a full wallet in my pocket, for all the weeks that I was in Burma. Sex there was, of course: a playful, charming, childish sex—a suffix or accessory, what condiments are in cooking, to the staunchness of our affection. He gave me everything he had: love, devotion, service, all his time and energy—and he was ready, too, to give me any sort of sexual entertainment, even the sorts he shrank from, had I asked for it, which I didn't. And I? What did I give him? I tried to lavish on him all the love and care that a friend, and a mother and father too, could be capable of; and for those few and short weeks we were happy, both of us. But trustworthy? Staunch? How could I pretend that my love was trustworthy when I had to leave him? Where in hell was its staunchness? And, may I be forgiven— but who can forgive the brutal perversities of this world?—I had to leave him. . . .

*   *   *

At first he slept at home—"home": the tiny hovel he shared with a horde of younger children and his overworked mother—too harrassed to find time for affection or even interest. Punctually he took back to her the "wages" I gave him; he was naïvely proud of giving his family more than he'd ever brought them before. With the equivalent of about three dollars he bought an old bicycle—before getting on to it he bunched his loonghi up through his crutch like a baby's nappy. When I moved from the hotel to the Pegu Club and had an outside room with its own front door in the compound behind, I madly took a chance and brought him to stay there. It was a stuffy British club whose members were government officials, bank managers, oil company executives, and the like—the most inappropriate audience one could think of in front of which to pop a small Burmese boy into one's bed. But the gamble came off: the club "boys," the servants, who knew Maung Tay Ba was my "bearer," took no notice of his being in and out of my room night as well as day; while the staid members, if they knew of his existence at all, showed no sign of curiosity. So he slept with me on what was little roomier than a camp-bed; lying sleeping against the white sheet his lemon-gold body was like the brass figure of a buddha—a buddha taking time off from meditation.

And buddhas were one of our pleasures: we loved to climb the long stairs up to the sanctuary of the golden Shwe Dagon pagoda, and idle among the multitude of silent images. I had my work to do, of course; sometimes I had to drive out to the little civil war that was being fought a dozen or so miles up country. But often I could managed a few hours free; and now and then a full day—then we would leave the city and make for that chain of lakes like pools of quicksilver that spread, among golden dunes and jade-and-emerald jungle, just north of Rangoon.

There were at least two staircases leading up to the Shwe Dagon shrines under the immense cupola of pure gold-leaf—perhaps there were four, one at each corner: that would accord with the regal grandeur of the place. At the bottom of the steps a notice announced: "Visitors must remove the footing"—one was required to take one's shoes off. I used to know how many steps there were up—it was a long climb; and all the way up one passed little stalls where things were sold: holy things, offerings, like posies of flowers and incense, touristic objects such as miniature buddhas and the unavoidable ebony elephants. At the top one came to the lofty and spacious loggia which, enclosed by stone balustrades, ran four-sided round the vast base of the golden dome; and formed four wide balconies projecting beneath and around it, from whose tiled pavement arose an ornate flowering— luxuriant yet orderly as an Italian garden, chaste as a Gothic vault—of pagodas in miniature, pinnacles and pyramidal turrets, all sheltering or embracing a sobering and mesmerising company of figures, of various sizes and in manifold postures, of gold or bronze or stone, and each of course representing the Buddha. Everywhere people were sweeping or dusting or cleaning, for it's obviously a blessing and an honour to perform such services for the Teacher; others were praying or sitting in attitudes of meditation, and others still walking about and chatting. Beneath the vast golden canopy I seem to remember an endless succession of chambers like stalls or stables or chancels or chapels: all surrounded by rows of silent, dominating images of the Buddha. Many contained also groups of saffron-clad boy-monks eating from their begging-bowls. I have stood with what reverence I can muster in in most kinds of places of worship, in the churches or temples or assemblies of most of the world's rites of religion; but I don't think I've ever known another place where I've experienced such an awareness of peace and gentleness and tranquillity of the spirit, such a feeling of meditative, or prayerful, if you like, power as I experienced among all those glorious musing idols of the golden Shwe Dagon—and I went there many times, and each time experienced the same anodyne sensations. On the way up, Maung Tay Ba would always buy himself a sprig of flowers which he would set up in the apropriate holder before whatever image he selected; and he would kneel down and hold up his hands palm to palm and look up sweetly at the impassive buddha. I don't think Maung Tay Ba was much of a practising buddhist, I'm sure he wasn't much given to devout exercises; but I never expect to see as pretty a praying again as his at the Shwe Dagon.

The road to the lakes seemed also the road to the end of the known world. It came to a stop on a wooded, sandy hill —sometimes a car would lose its grip in the sand and its wheels would whir and bore deeper down. Among the trees was a tea-shop and snack-bar; people, mostly Burmese, would come out here on holidays from the city for a picnic or an hour's fresh air. But nobody went further: beyond was wilderness: water, sand, and rank greenery—a tangle of undergrowth and stunted jungle trees rioting over the dunes.

We used to get provisions at the tea-shop: sandwiches, fruit, some cold boiled rice, bottles of lemonade; and hire a boat from the proprietor, a small sampan; and then we'd set off for the day, lazily along the narrow waterways, snaking and meandering between the verdurous dunes, through channels which, like widening rivulets approaching an estuary, gradually opened into the breathless silvery expanse of the lake. We'd row unhurriedly, without much thinking about it, so that we could apply all our faculties to the sheer enjoyment of being where we were, of being naked in the warm shining air (we had taken our clothes off the first moment we could), and of being together. The sampan moved forward in leisurely thrusts, like an elderly breast-stroke-swimmer's; and the creaking of the oars against the tholes seemed like an answer to the waterbirds uttering their lonely cries above us.

"You stay with me?" he would ask—though it seemed more an assertion than a question. "You not leave Burma?" And I would answer, with my heart breaking and my sense of truth rebelling against what I knew to be a lie. "I shall stay —or if I have to go away, I shall come back." This exchange was constantly being repeated on all our excursions, during all our nights, in between all our daily doings. "You stay with me?"—or sometimes, "Me stay with you?" . . .

Once out in the wide lagoon we would head for a long low sandbank which we called "our" island and which, from a distance, seemed to brush the surface of the water like a streak of saffron. With a final scurry of the oars we'd run the boat's stem into the sand and jump ashore. . . . He'd run about and dance and leap, turn somersaults and cartwheels, do hand-springs and back jumps and every kind of acrobatics that his mind could think of and his limbs prompt him to. . . . And I'd watch him, and ask myself how it could be possible for such loveliness to exist. . . . The lemon-gold of his skin seemed almost the same colour as the sand he danced upon; so that the gyrations of his prancing body became like the flicker and sheen of sunlight on an amber floor.

And rowing back he would say. "You stay with me? You not go?" And as we neared again the narrowing channels and the green-covered dunes, the falling sun reflected from the west would begin to turn the water red.

As my mind had always known it would, though my heart pretended it wouldn't, the cable from London came: I was to leave at once for Singapore, and after a short while there, move on. . . . Where could a small Burmese boy be fitted into this programme of duty and the wretched earning of a livelihood?

In those days, so long ago now, a flying-boat which moored in the Rangoon River was the means of getting in and out of Burma by air. One went down some steps from the official buildings on the river bank to a landing stage below, and a small launch took one across to the aircraft. I remember the absurd formality Mauny Tay Ba had to submit to before they would allow him to come with me on to the pier: he had to be searched by customs in case he were carrying something illicit to pass to me after I myself had been cleared—him, searched by Customs, with nothing but his cotton-thin sarong and his bare lemon-gold skin.

He stood beside me and sobbed—sobbed like a child that's being taken away from its mother, like a boy being hauled off to some school. "You come back? You not leave me?" he kept asking between his sobs. "You promise?"

"I'll come back," I said. "I promise."

When it was time for me to get into the launch he cried out desperately: "You promise? You promise?" and as the launch was pushed off and turned its nose into midstream I could still hear his call: "You come back? You promise?"

From the porthole window by my seat I watched his lemon-pale breast and shoulders and arms, and the ankle-length brown loonghi below them. Even at that distance I could see how his tiny face was screwed up and his shoulders shaking. The plane scudded off over the water and rose, circling over the landing-stage and that minute figure below. The other passengers were staring at me: it was my turn to be sobbing—tears were running down my face and I was crying out loud, and, absurdly, I couldn't find my handkerchief.

I broke my promise. Once again, as so often in my life, the world I was caught up in was stronger than free will. I never went back.

NAPLES

It MAY well be that the naughty population of Naples is greater in proportion to her virtuous population than that of any other great city not particularly noted for puritanism. If this be so, the reasons are pretty easy to detect and are to be found, like most such reasons, in history—in that curious Rabelaisian rabble which, half-naked, half-starved and wholly rascally, rather paradoxically provided the most zealous support for the Neapolitan monarchy at the time of the Napoleonic wars; and in the fact that at least two hundred years ago Naples became a principal goal of that incorrigible corrupter, the international tourist, and has remained one ever since. At the end of the eighteenth century and the beginning of the next, the *lazzaroni* (the Neapolitan name for the cohorts of lighthearted vagabonds who lived in the gutters and gaily performed every kind of outrage and obscenity in the public streets and whose children were bred to picturesque villainy) were the King's most loyal subjects and consequently enjoyed his special affection and many privileges—he fully understood their ways of life, himself cheerfully defecating along with his courtiers among the Farnese Marbles stacked like rubbish in the corridors of the Royal Palace. No wonder, then, that the *lazzaroni* and their descendants have during two hundred years become skilled in the arts of swindling, diddling and victimizing in a dozen different ways, with or without violence, the swarms of foreign tourists who year after year come into their town with pockets full of money. One cannot blame them: it's in their blood, the heritage of their history: no more than one can blame a prince for succeeding to his father's throne. A stranger in Naples should be careful; although it's a city where one may make the best of friends, it is, too, a place where rashness can bring painful regret and the delights of temptation turn damnably sour. I was taught a first lesson in 1952; and, not having taken it properly to heart, was given a second lesson a few years later.

My first lesson took the form of a financial transaction : I fell for one of the oldest tricks done by the Neapolitan con-boys since paper currency took the place of coins. Going southward along the pillared frontage of the royal palace, past all those marble kings, you come out of the square on to a high esplanade looking down upon some dusty gardens and beyond to the quays and shipping of the port. Jutting over the road's supporting masonry, there's a walled "belvedere" from which on can survey the full pictorial drama of Vesuvius and, through the sparkling blue haze of the Bay, the grand sweep of the coast and the Sorrentine hills. There is also in summer, for those who want a change from scenery, the spectacle just below of the *lazzaroni,* or their juvenile descendants, bathing shamelessly unclad from a crumbling jetty. Here naturally tourists are apt to linger; and here too come the professional diddlers of tourists.

Here I was one glorious July morning, during my very first stay in Naples, leaning over the wall and gazing at the boys bathing below. A pleasant-looking young man came and stood beside me and, after the inevitable "Hey Joe—you spik Ingleesh?" began talking with such kindly courtesy that I at once felt I could trust his candid smile and forgive his egregious English. He was willing—indeed eager, he explained in his ingratiatingly convincing yankeefied film-ganster slang—to pay 200 lire above the official rate of exchange for every English pound-note he could buy. His explanation was quite simple, and so plausible : he earned an honest living by going aboard British ships in the harbour, buying from the sailors all the English cigarettes he could get, and selling them at a good profit on the black market—so I could understand, couldn't I, why he would pay well for all the English currency he could get? Of course I understood, I said; and I thought what a good idea this was— I'd be making a nice profit for myself (don't we all like "getting a good exchange?") and also I'd be doing a good turn to this nice enterprising young man who had such an open, frank expression. I had two five-pound notes in a pocket and pulled them out—and suddenly two or three friends had appeared and were crowding round me, jostling and flustering, while I was given what was plainly a roll of thousand-lire notes in exchange for my fivers. My friend went off, while his companions continued to crowd me against the wall for a few seconds; then they too slipped quickly away—and I had a look at my fat handful of Italian money. Rolled into the outer 1,000-lire note were twenty or so pieces of newspaper, perfectly cut to size.

How can any grown man be so stupid, I'd say, if it'd happened to anybody else—they wouldn't catch me like that! But they would, and they did; and so deft is their skill, so plausible their manner, they go on catching tourists with this simple dodge and will, doubtless, continue to do so as long as there are tourists to be caught.

But there's another way of catching the tourist, or any foreigner, or, now and then probably, the native too; but the field here is smaller, the market limited: a special kind of tourist is required, though this kind is in pretty constant supply—it's the paedophile tourist who's caught here, the boy-lover.

Several years after my lesson from the currency-exchange experts, when I was no longer a simple tourist but actually living in Naples—when, that is, I thought I knew my way about, wise to all the usual Neapolitan tricks—I was desultorily rambling one genial summer evening and strayed, foolishly as I should have known, into the famous—or notorious— Galleria Umberto, that huge cruciform crystal palace that rears itself magniloquently opposite the San Carlo opera-house. It was an evening of *festa,* I remember, though I forget what it honoured, and the streets were packed with people and the sort of noise that crowds enjoying themselves make. It was one of those evenings when one feels inside one a glow of expectant elation; an evening of soft warmth, dead still, yet freshened from the sea : when one has had a few glasses of wine and knows there are more ahead : when one is light-hearted and fond of one's fellow-beings, and ready for its finale. And, as one saunters through the thronging people, so many enchanting and suggestive faces are about that the imagination becomes aflame and one drops all desires but one. . . .

The *Galleria* is an enormous and ornate structure of glass, cast-iron and marble, real or assumed, conceived with the industrial-romantic idealism of late nineteenth-century railroad-station architecture. Four wide and lofty arcades, with moulded, arching ceilings, meet like the arms of a cross beneath an immense glass dome and form at their other extremities, north, south, east and west, four splendid portals on to four different streets in the "nitelife" part of the city. Along the sides of the arcades are gift shops offering overpriced trinkets to tourists, and a dozen or more coffee-bars with tables and chairs set pleasantly out on the flagstones—it's amusing at any time of the day to sit here for a while and watch the Neapolitan world go by. Even early in the morning, these arcades are paced earnestly in twos or threes by shabbily genteel *signori* who, by the important way they carry their briefcases and the condescension with which they bow to acquaintances, make it clear that in their own view at least they're men of consequence; while larger groups of other men, worrying less about what sort of figure they're cutting than what figures their companions are quoting, are vociferously doing business among themselves—but I've never been able to discover what their business is : they look like a conclave of déclassé stockbrokers. Towards lunchtime the tourists come, to drink at the café tables, look in the shop windows and comment on the strollers; and to the strollers are added a few elegant tarts who exchange pleasantries with the waiters and seem, on their haughty high heels, to tittup along in an aura of challenging virtue. Now and then a boy passes languidly, with long bare brown legs under a pair of tight knickers and dark eyes roving beneath provocative lashes. Through a couple of low archways in the arcades one may venture into a dim, cavernous world which leads, down echoing stairs, to a subterranean labyrinth of halls and corridors where daylight can never enter but which resound with the cries of lighthearted—and largely light-fingered—youth : it's a world of billiard saloons and one-armed bandits and pintable halls and one or two very cheap cinemas—a world patronized, naturally, by the less honourable sections of the adolescent classes. But from the impeccable paving of the

64

Galleria itself one could never guess that this louche world existed beneath one's feet—so veritably an "underworld."

On that evening I'm writing of, the four arcades of the Galleria were packed tight with people of all sorts excited by the mass-infection of gaiety which the fact of *fiesta* always mysteriously spreads. A military band was playing under the crystal cupola—the band, I think it was, of the *carabinieri,* that super-police force which on gala occasions wears eighteenth-century uniforms. The crowds came and went and pushed and jostled and glided and slid like a pond brimful of swimming live sardines. I managed to find a chair outside one of the cafés—the only café there which sold ordinary wine as well as liqueurs and coffee. So I sipped my glass of heady, acid white wine, and watched the throng seething before me like a gentle brew of colourfully mixed vegetables. Suddenly I saw, standing at the edge of the crowd and staring fixedly at me, a pretty boy of about fifteen with brownish fair hair and the apple cheeks and blue eyes of some far-off Northern ancestry. But what struck me about his appearance was its superlative respectability: not only was his charming face a picture of innocence and honesty, but his clothes were just what a prosperous middle-class father would want his son to wear. His neat brown suit was nicely made, and he even wore a Sunday-best collar and tie—and there were still a few years to go before the economic "Italian miracle" became reflected in the excellent mass-produced clothes worn today even by the children of the Southern poor. This, I thought to myself, is too good to miss; although I'm seldom attracted to the sons of the bourgeoisie. Yet in Naples, common sense told me, a face however framed—and a delightful face into the bargain—which is beaming with the light of candour like the guileless candles of a Christmas tree isn't often found—and what could the fixity of that lucent stare mean but a desire for friendship? I beckoned him to join me; and after a Coca Cola for him and another glass of wine for me, we went out into the Via Roma—the "Toledo" as it's still popularly called —and crossed over to the entrance to the funicular. With a delightfully confiding smile, he had instantly agreed that we should go to my lodging on the Vomero.

Three funicular railways take one to the top of those splendid slopes around whose feet the city sits and whose

65

crown is the Castel Sant'Elmo. Each starts from a different district of the city below and ends in a separate part of the township above—the Vomero is a big hilltop suburb with an atmosphere and appearance that's almost foreign to Naples proper; my apartment there was so hard to find and the approaches to the Vomero were so varied, that I'd always supposed nobody who'd been there once would ever find his way again.

My new companion that evening was charming in every way: amusing, well-mannered, obliging and most friendly; although his interest in the evening's principal entertainment seemed to me vaguely insipid—I thought perhaps this was due to shyness. He displayed a remarkable reluctance to take the little present I proffered when we said "arrivederci" (for, of course, I begged him to meet me again the next evening) and only accepted it when I was absolutely insistent. All my first impressions of him seemed to be confirmed. I wonder why I've entirely forgotten his name? Is it because disaster, like a merciful india-rubber, sometimes erases from one's memory the evidences of one's sillier mortifications?

The next evening we met, as arranged, at the Metropolitano cinema, which is just off, so far as I remember, the famous Via Chiaia. After watching a picture we went again to the Vomero, this time taking the funicular from the Piazza Amedeo; and again I had difficulty in persuading him to take my modest gift. The third evening, he said—though the reasons he gave me weren't at all clear—we must meet again outside the Metropolitano and at an hour just after dusk: we wouldn't go to any movie, he insisted, but straight up to the Vomero. Okay by me, I answered; ready to fall in with any plans this charming person might propose.

How clearly it all returned to me, back in Naples five years later when I went to the Metropolitano to see the first showing there of the film of *Il Gattopardo*—"The Leopard"....

Happily, buoyantly, I walked that evening beside him to the funicular station. What a lucky man I am, I remember thinking! Which fairy benefactress at my cradle can have ordained that I should at that precise moment in the Galleria encounter this immaculate creature! He chatted as gaily as always as we ambled along, and seemed even more carefree and winning than he'd previously been. I did notice that he glanced a couple of times over his shoulder—or rather, I remembered afterwards that I'd noticed it: at the time I just thought: what a pretty toss of the head!—I was a million miles from the idea of a tiny sly reconnaissance.

An echoing stone stairway took us up to my one-room-and-a-shower apartment on the second floor; I could hear any ordinary footsteps coming up a flight away. I had two doors: an outer landing-door and then, through a tiny hallway, the door to my room; both shut on a spring latch. I led the way in: "Shut the doors after you, won't you," I said over my shoulder as I was switching on the lights—and afterwards I remembered that I hadn't heard the click of either latch. It's extraordinary how minute details, unobserved at the time for their presence or absence, are often brought back to one later by some mental jolt—drawn up by drama from the cellars of the mind as tiny fragments of evidence are revealed by forensic ruthlessness.

He lit up a cigarette, but hadn't even time to take his jacket off before they walked in, all three of them. They must have come up those flights of steps as softly as foxes: I hadn't heard a sound, although both doors were ajar. But there was plenty to hear when they'd come in—with the heart-stopping unexpectedness of a thunderclap in a cloudless sky. One of them started shouting at me, while the other two set about the boy. There was a good deal of Neapolitan dialect in their Italian, but I got the gist of what they were saying. "They're his brothers, see," said the one to me. "They've come to teach him a lesson for doing this, and to put you where you ought to be—in gaol. *Hai capito?*—understand?" Meanwhile, the other two were giving the boy what seemed to me an awful doing over, punching him and savagely smacking his face—his whimpering and blubbering sounded so convincing that I felt suddenly more sorry for him than for myself: "Leave the boy alone," I started shouting, "it's not his fault." But they went on pummelling him, and while they pummelled they scolded: Dirty whore, he was, going with filthy foreigners, they said; dishonouring the family—and his own dishonour had got to be avenged; the foreigner had got to make amends —if he dishonoured the family by letting filthy foreigners touch him, the filthy foreigners must pay, to put his honour

67

right . . . *e così via,* and so on and so on, as the Italians say. . . .

Suddenly the pummelling stopped, and so did the blubbering: the boy calmly brushed his hair back and straightened his tie; the signs of pain slid from his face like melting snow from a roof. Then all four turned to me, and the chief "brother" told me, waving his arms and shoving his nose almost against mine, that I must redeem the boy's honour, and his family's, by paying up, or else we'd all proceed in a body to the police—there was a lot of talk about the boy's being *minorenne* : under age. But it didn't take much worldly wisdom to tell me that the threat of the police was bluff; what frightened me was the probability of my being beaten up by three well-grown toughs and one growing assistant. I wasted no time arguing: Go through all my pockets, I said: that's absolutely all I've got here. I knew I had a five thousand-lire note, and a thousand-lire—the latter intended for the boy's honorarium. And that's all they found, after searching all my clothes. The chief "brother" pocketed the booty, gave a quick look round the room and jerked his head towards the door. *Andiamo,* he muttered, and they filed softly out. The boy was the last to go; he turned for a moment to display on his sweet face a mocking mixture of a sneer and a leer. It was a sneer I certainly deserved.

I've never understood why they left so tamely, and with such a poor haul—no more than ten dollars. If they'd looked in a drawer under some handkerchiefs, they'd have found fifty thousand lire, which would have made their evening's trouble worthwhile. And I doubt whether the boy got even half the thousand I was going to give him.

One must watch one's step very carefully in Naples. And yet there are such enchanting friends to be made in that gorgeous city of contrariness: Vincenzo's companionship, of long ago, is one that comes to mind. . . .

TANGIER

THE TANGIER of those days, a writer may feel, was a city for which there weren't enough adjectives. To describe successfully the purulent and prurient and paradoxical life of that grotesque city, to depict the astonishing farrago of a society from its touristical surface of oriental romance to its murkiest sump of multifarious evil, would require an extravagance of vocabulary and a lushness of phrase beyond the resources of most writers—there never was, surely, a town so enthrallingly wicked, unless Babylon and Gomorrah could live up to its high standard of depravity; or so fascinatingly motley and mongrel and miscellaneous, unless indeed Babel was what it's proverbially supposed to have been.

Nearly every appetite could have been satiated here—though an appetite for art and the pleasures of the mind would hardly even be satisfied. Only one human desire had little hope of being fulfilled at all : the desire for love. Tangier was a city without love—or so it seemed to me at the time of which I'm writing : just before the war and for a year during it, and again in 1947–48 when I lived there as a journalist.

But the town and "zone" had everything else (Tangier was then an internationalized segment of Morocco—the "International Zone") : luxuriousness and all the sensual pleasures human invention can think up, and an agreeably oriental sense of personal irresponsibility; enough squalor in every shade of leprous variation to please the most gothic-minded romanticist; "007"-type espionage of a generally non-lethal sort and in the main comfortably fictional; smuggling of anything illegal from cigarettes and drugs to State secrets, from blocked capital to hunted criminals or political refugees;

every kind of intrigue and fraud and fiddle and law-evasion. At a time of wartime restrictions and warring currencies, I saw cheques on New York, London, Paris, Berlin and so on being sold by auction in a mid-morning movie-theatre ("I have here escudos twenty-four thousand and fifteen centavos on Lisbon. . . ."); and an abundant market for the supply of almost any off-beat or illicit sexual demand, from small girls and boys to pregnant Negresses and Arabs with out-size genitals. . . . But it was a city without love. The odours of lust, like the fumes of liquor, hung in every street; but if you insisted on love you were given a poor effigy of it and made to pay heavily.

The town was too much of a flea-market for love. All the goods were second-hand, or damaged, or made for a quick turnover and a quick get-away. Nothing ever seemed quite genuine : one walked through the town with the feeling of being an extra in some ham melodrama, entering into such absurd situations as, during the war, finding oneself sitting on a café terrace beside German Nazis, Italian Fascists and Spanish Falangists—a situation which, to one born and bred on the Allied side, presented difficult problems of etiquette; or meeting some ludicrous "neutral" acquaintance, known to be a "spy" for both sides, who says : "I've just come from the German legation—I'm on my way to the British. . . ." Even the retired British colonels who lived grandly on the Mountain, and the solid bourgeois householders of the Marshan, acquired a semblance of phoneyness merely from the fact that they had chosen to live in Tangier. In the Kasbah, nobody could call Barbara Hutton phoney, or her money; but one could say unusual. . . . There were plenty of bogus barons and dubious duchesses : even the family of the Marquess of Bute, who owned a quantity of the town, seemed to have something of the theatrical unreality of the rest of the Tangerine nobility. Every day, almost, was a holiday— yet like the Eve of a Tangerine St. Bartholomew, so curiously precarious did existence feel, founded upon so much that was spurious. Friday, of course, was the Muslim day of rest, Saturday the Jewish and Sunday the Christian, and nearly every other day of the week was generally a saint's day or a feast of some sort belonging to one of the three—or else a "national day" of one of the members of the Zone's administering condominium.

Like the hard, metallic sunshine and the cutting winds of the winter, life in Tangier seemed to have no soft corners for the gentler emotions—indeed, for emotions at all, except those like anger or jealousy. Everything had a price and had to be bargained for; all was "business" and business hasn't any room for tenderness. That's why, I suppose, among all the boys I knew there—Arab, Berber, Jewish, Portuguese, Spanish, French—I remember none with a pang: I can scarcely remember any of their names—though I can recall the outlines of some of their physical attributes. . . . They were most of them charming, if some of them were charmingly mercenary; but none displayed affection or really aroused it: it was all commerce, though a commerce nearly always spiced with piquancy and pleasure, like buying something very beautiful in an antique-shop or finding a long-craved book on a second-hand stall.

I remember a fifteen-year-old Spanish boy, tall and slim, with long, lank hair and delicate feline limbs; I met him on the *playa*, the broad ribbon of white sand that sweeps like a high road round the shore of Tangier bay. On his second visit he brought his next younger brother, aged thirteen, explaining that the earlier the boy learned about the ways of the world the better. He himself had been taught by an older brother—there were three more little brothers yet to grow to the right age, the youngest still an infant.

I remember a Jewish boy, dark and softly handsome like an Andalusian, whose memory in my mind's eye still brings back his name—Moise: he was a "superior" local Jew who spoke French rather than Jewish-Arabic. He used to take me to a curious bathing establishment kept in their back-yard by a Jewish family (there were a number of similar establishments to be found in that sombre jungle of slums behind the Petit Socco). It was meant for one bather (or two) and consisted of a small *pisé* hut like a potting-shed in which was placed a cauldron of hot water, scrubbing brushes and other ablutionary instruments; and a tiny walled yard open to the sky in which to dry oneself in the sun. To one of these Moise brought me, and we scrubbed each other with the brushes, and made playful love in the sunshine. . . .

71

There was another Jew : a sweet, shy fourteen-year old with red-ochre-dark hair and a fair clear northern skin. He was diffident and gentle-mannered; yet every evening, one week of summer, he sat on my back door step which I rarely used; until one warm dusk, I happened to look out that way, and there he was . . . sitting shyly on the big stone step, with his short knickers rolled back over his thighs and his bare knees and calves white in the twilight. We talked that first evening; the second, I think it was, I sat beside him on the step; and on the third I stroked his knee and warm and silky expanse of thigh. On the fourth evening, he came indoors. . . .

And Dris—or was his name Abderhamman? A tall, long-boned Arab who may've been any age between twelve and sixteen, whose huge melancholy eyes were like black olives set in the parchment of his face, and who with his cowled head looked like an Italian-Primitive saint, so elongated did his narrow-shouldered figure appear within the gracile fluting of his ankle-length *jellaba*. I found him on the *playa*; on the stretch of sand, backed by the ranks of bathing cabins and beach-bars, where in summer a profusion of half-nude European women lay baking in the sun, like lengths of washed-up seaweed : each the unembarrassed centre of a ring of Arab or Berber youths hungrily whetting their imaginations upon all the female flesh they could see. He was squatting with his legs crossed beneath the skirts of his *jellaba* and his hands thrust deep through the slits at the sides; his head was huddled under his cowl as if he were cold; but I could see the sad, stoical passion of his black eyes and his half-opened magenta lips. And then I apprehended an almost imperceptible motion, as miniature as the throbbing in a lizard's throat, which was infinitesimally vacillating the fabric of his robe above his lap—he was, I saw in a gust of realization, quietly and covertly flogging himself beneath the tractable shrouds of his robe. . . .

I recall too that small Berber, blue-eyed and tousled, with the impish air of a London urchin, whom I found one late night alone on the deserted *playa* : a hot night of summer, when the sky was incandescent with stars and even the moonlight looked warm. In this silvered darkness, the water's edge seemed an infinite distance from the far side of the beach, above which the dunes hung like purple banks of obscurity; apart from the lights of the town, sparkling up the hillside as if from another planet, we might have been alone on a desert island. We took off our clothes and bathed together naked and blissful, in the warm, soft, unmoving water—I remember how the moonlight made his white body look like freshly polished marble. And after our bathe, because his *douar* was some way out in the countryside and he had nowhere to sleep, I took him back to my villa.

There was a French boy—his name was Raoul. It started with our playing chess; his parents had taken a villa for the holidays much nearer the *playa* than mine—a tumbledown cliff-cottage on the sea side of the Marshan—and we used to play at their villa. They were very self-consciously middle-class people : the father was a municipal personage—*directeur des jardins publiques* of a big provincial town. While the father and mother were dozing in their deck-chairs on the beach, with newspapers over their faces, Raoul and I would be amusing ourselves on the matrimonial bed.

A black-haired Portuguese boy, I recall, with skin the colour of drying orange-peel : I came upon him solemnly masturbating among the sand-dunes near the railway station —he was taking a short-cut between the fishing-boat quay and the market; beside him on the sand, while he was at it, lay his basket of gleaming fresh fish. He told me he tossed himself off regularly three or four times a day : whenever, in fact he found himself with his hands idle and in sufficient privacy. . . . Those dunes, deep and steep as quarries, their sandy crests greenish with growths of scrub or coarse camel-grass, their depths hidden from casual sight until, arriving at the very edge, one looked down . . . these dunes, austerely remote, one would think, from human peccadillos, the haunt of seagulls and aged mystics repeating the ninety-nine names of God among the sandy solitudes, yet sometimes revealed quaint surprises to the random wanderer. Once, in the month of Ramadan, when every adult and near-adult Muslim must by law refrain during the hours of daylight from eating, drinking, smoking and sex—in other words, from any class of sensuality at all—I greatly alarmed an unfortunate Negro youth by coming upon him while, deep in the shelter of one of these sandy caverns, he was eating a huge slice of water-melon with his right hand—thus eating and drinking at the same time—and with his left fondling and massaging a hefty black penis. He was thus committing three crimes together—and what's more, at the very moment when the *mueddin* from the nearest minaret was wailing the midday call to prayer; the young man's grin of relief when he saw that I was an infidel unlikely to denounce him to the police was charming. . . . On another day I chanced upon the unusual spectacle of a childish exercise in bestiality : a lanky fair-haired boy of about fifteen—Spanish he turned out to be—was holding with one hand a large mongrel bitch by the tail (he had her well-trained) while, his eyes fixed upon the vaginal orifice, he worked away at himself with the other; when I unexpectedly came upon the scene he dropped the dog like a hot brick, but was too far gone to stop the other hand. . . . This was, as it happens, the only time in my life that I encountered an experiment in bestiality; though it is of course common in Morocco and probably other Arab countries among country boys : Moorish friends in Rabat told me that small boys normally copulate with the female donkeys in their charge, in the belief that this makes the penis grow. . . But those splendid sand-dunes, full of a strange unworldly beauty and full, often, of strange adventure, alas no longer exist. When I was in Tangier four or five years ago, I found that they were being built over, for some industrial purpose I suppose.

Clearly, of course, I remember Manolo and his bosom friend Pedro; I can see Manolo's blond Catalonian profile, with the golden down on his chin and cheeks; and the Saracenic Semiticism of Pedro's Spanish good looks. They'd both be getting on for thirty-five years of age today—and fondly possessing, I hope, large and growing families. Why, they may have sons of just the age I knew them at! For a time they composed my "crew" aboard a fifteen-foot double-ender I had converted into a makeshift cabin-cruiser and lived in at her moorings among the fishing fleet. They were happy, pleasant companions when for the moment they had everything they wanted to eat and smoke and had forgotten to wheedle something extra out of me—they were such a decorative pair and so entertaining that for a short time their companionship was worth paying for even at their exorbitant rates. One of our favourite excursions was round to that immense expanse of empty sand, acres of superb desert, on the Atlantic side: beyond the classic rocks known as the Pillars of Hercules; whose rolling, pitted sands—which, with miniature ravines and stony *wadis,* were like a model of the Sahara—ultimately merged with the Atlantic, with its white curls of breakers endlessly unrolling on the shore like coils of molten netting. Nobody was here, except for a rare striding Berber going to his *douar* of huts somewhere or other, or a tiny pigtailed boy shrilly calling to his goats. Nobody was here, nobody: it was a kind of Atlantic "Empty Quarter"; and here the three of us, naked as the day we were born, swam and ran and played ball and basked and explored the caves of Hercules: I wonder where all those photographs I took have got to? . . . I have heard recently that today there stands on the sands of that old desert by the Pillars of Hercules a "lido" with snack-bars and striped umbrellas and juke-boxes and all the proper tourist attractions.

Late at night, before dragging oneself from the temptations of the town and going home to bed, one would have just one more drink on the pavement of the Petit Socco (or Zoco Chico), the minuscule quadrangle whose Spanish charm was enhanced by a ban on all wheeled traffic; and here a half-dozen or so of Jewish shoeshine boys would offer themselves for the night—one had merely to take one's pick. . . . Behind this little square, at whose café tables half the business of the town, licit or furtive, was conducted by the droves of commission-agents, middlemen and "couriers" who always seemed to be in the middle of any business deal, lay a tangle of narrow streets, dark and mainly dirty, which formed the old European-Jewish quarter—the new "French" town and the ancient Muslim fastness of the Kasbah seemed to belong to different worlds. In these old sombre streets most of Tangier's orthodox sin was housed—I remember in those old days two "hotels" delightfully named Hotel Satan and Hotel Delirium. It was in one of these streets that one night I met, thinking it was a boy, an Arab girl of about twelve: in the male *jellaba* she wore (in those days no respectable woman or girl wore out-of-doors anything but the all-enveloping white *haik*) it was impossible to think she wasn't a boy. In one of these streets, too, there lived the Spanish girl of twelve or perhaps thirteen who, for a time, took to haunting my doorstep, when I lived in the town, after she'd been told, quite wrongly, that I liked little girls; she always brought with her on these visits her ten-year-old sister. There was an Englishman there at the time, a highly respected figure in the Zone, who was known to all the boys within miles as "Mister Bob"—simple masturbation was his pleasure, for which as every boy in town knew, he paid a set fee. I was walking one day near the harbour when a Spanish boy who was approaching, knowing that I was a friend of this man's, suddenly began jerking his hand up and down in front of him in a masturbatory movement and exclaiming loudly, "Mister Bob! Mister Bob!" as if this were a street-cry advertising his wares—apparently "Mister Bob" had become the English synonym in the boys' vocabulary for sexual business. . . .

Such was the Tangier which I knew twenty-five or thirty years ago. It was a city where a visitor out for a riotous time could plunge into the best-stocked pool of exotic pleasures outside the Arabian Nights and believe he had reached Paradise; but for a resident, for someone who *lived* there, it was different. A stay there for some time worked like a long period of too much cigarette-smoking : the poison of corruption, like that of nicotine, engendered a growing nausea : there came a moment when a resident, gasping for clean air, longed to leave. But the fascination of the place was such that one always longed to get back again.

Nowadays it's changed. A decade of independence and nationalist politico-prudery has led to the expulsion of some of the more flagrant customers of girls and boys and the closing of the more shameless bars. But many more decades will be needed to change the course of a centuries-old tradition of cupidity and corruption, in whose spoils a half-dozen races share; and I dare say one can still have a good time there.

TOKYO

THE SWIMMING-POOL in Hibiya Park in Tokyo, as I recall it, was a spirited and apt construction whose vaguely classic mood chimed in well with the verdant formality of its surroundings. It must have escaped the bombardments: even Japanese enterprise and ingenuity couldn't have built such a delightful luxury so soon after the catastrophe of defeat; and at a time of political bewilderment and economic despair and while their every action was ruled by the American "occupation-naires," as the soldiers and officials and camp-followers of General Douglas MacArthur's army of occupation were known.

At one end of the pool, I seem to remember, there rose from the greenery of the gardens a tall screen of masonry or concrete, concave in design, resembling perhaps the *postscaenium* of a Roman theatre and giving to the whole plan something of a sense of ritual. But while the *postscaenium* of antiquity concealed the dressing-rooms behind the stage, here the changing area was at the other end of the bath and not concealed at all; it was a wide, airy shelter opening straight on to the water and in full view of the public who daily, in summer, gathered along the barriers of netting which enclosed the pool, to watch the boys disporting themselves on the diving boards like sleek, swift, black-headed darting arrows. Here in this shelter, as if on a brightly lighted stage, with any passers-by for audience, plus the girls splashing in the pool (the girls had, I think, a separate shelter to change in, scarcely less public), the boys arriving for a swim stripped their clothes off and meticulously wound about themselves—in between the buttocks, under the scrotum, round the waist and down

77

again—the length of flimsy scarlet sash which they twisted about their person with the dexterity of an Arab wrapping his turban; until, naked except for this trim whisp of scarlet enveloping their genitals, these boys resembled delicate slim-boned versions of the classical Japanese wrestler depicted in so many traditional prints.

Outside one never knew quite what one's eyes might catch. One breathless afternoon, a short way from the bathing place, I came upon two sylph-like youngsters, slender and elegant as Tanagra figurines and with gleaming wet skin as white as daisies' petals after rain : they were standing, still dripping from the pool, on a diminutive knoll, contrived with the cunning of the landscape gardener, from whose summit rose a kind of Nipponized Palladian pagoda in miniature, a charming piece of ornamental nonsense which added to the formal lawns and walks and shrubberies a pleasant touch of eighteenth-century fantasy. The boys, I suppose, had come there to dry themselves in the sun and bask : the dressing shelter had been in shadow. And there, beside the toy edifice of monumental concrete, perched upon this endearing little theatrical hillock, the two of them slowly unwound their scarlet fig-leaves with all the titillatory dilatoriness of the deliberate strip-teaser—until they stood stark naked on the municipal sward, for all the world as if two cockney boys were surprised nude beside the Albert Memorial. The effect was wonderfully felicitous : a blend of the classical and the rococo: an eighteenth-century engraving of an Arcadian romp, with a touch of what one might call the chinoiserie so popular at the Courts of Europe during the last decades of the seventeen-hundreds.

I met Kishi in this park. I couldn't guess, that first day, that this meeting was to be the inauguration of one of the four great loves of my entire life : I had supposed, at first, that fate had found me an exceptionally attractive ephemeron—but it turned out to be bigger than the entire universe. Mine has been a peripatetic life : it has generally been my aim, and sometimes my achievement, as I moved about the map, to discover as soon as possible after arrival in a new place a boy companion whom I could be happy with as long as I stayed there, and even longer—thus satisfying that insistent need *to love* (much more important than *being loved*) and saving

78

all the bother of searching. This, by the grace of Izanami and the rest of the Shinto gods, is what happened to me in Japan; and consequently I found out nothing about the paedophilist world of Tokyo—although, I believe, there was plenty to be found out, and a great deal right under one's nose. I therefore saw no boy-brothel, though I don't doubt there were numbers to be found; in the frenetic and tinselled Ginza, that surprising thoroughfare of rich shops and cheap-jack street stalls, I saw no red-mouthed and sunken-eyed boy-whores; I exploited none of the homeless war-waifs who haunted the subterranean mysteries of the central railway station. Nothing of that sort did I look for (I've often wondered what a wealth of thrills I may have missed!); and saw nothing to demonstrate, what I'd been assured, that Tokyo was the gayest city in the East. But what was shown by my meeting with Kishi was this : in Tokyo there was love for the boy-lover; and even sexual frolics with ordinary boys like Kishi's friends were entirely free of corruption. I was lucky, surely : Tokyo to me—this teeming, hideous city of millions, suffering from the neuroses of despair, demoralized and depraved by war and defeat and submission to foreign occupation—Tokyo to me meant love, and no breath of corruption. Indeed I was lucky; but I had to pay a high price for my luck—the agonizing cost, which the boy-lover so often has to pay of saying goodbye.

*　　　*　　　*

In the evening, after I'd filed my story for the day, I'd go to his mother's restaurant for fried rice and beer : I always asked for fried rice there—it became a joke that sent her into eddies of toothy chuckles. Perhaps "restaurant" is a name rather above its station : it was a small eating-house for working men, very cheap but always clean, where one ate a good simple meal—rice, soups, and simply done fish and meat. The place seemed to thrive; the destruction of war was being busily succeeded by reconstruction—and, besides, the Japanese economy was by 1950 working for the Americans in Korea. I ate in the family rooms above the shop, while Kishi's little brothers and sisters played on the floor beside me. Then, after supper, we'd drive to our home—"our" home, because his mother had "given" him to me. "Do you want him?" Mama-

San had asked, "I'll give him to you"; while Kishi translated in his schoolroom English. At first, until we found our house, we stayed in a small Japanese hotel: a tiny place possessed of a sort of fairyland charm for one whose ideas of Japan came from childhood picturebooks and stories—here, in real life, was the Japanese house of my childhood: a place of such delicacy and refinement that one wanted to speak softly and be gentle in all one's movements. Our room was of the usual elegant simplicity: the sliding walls, tapestry-hung and mute; the piles of downy, silky, voluptuous bedding stowed in noiseless, invisible lockers, the inches-high table for our tea or meals; the steaming delicate food in fragile cups and bowls and the wooden Japanese chopsticks, to be thrown away after the meal. And, above everything in my memory, the *tatami* flooring: that paragon of matting, mossy and springy and warm, blissful to lie on or to walk over barefooted; inviting and restful to look at; the quintessence of comfort and refined and imaginative practicality; the symbol of that good taste and style, of the elegancies and felicities of an exquisitely miniature manner of living, which were uniqely old Japan's and which, God forgive the West, are being obliterated by the sweep of Western vulgarization that started after the war with the American occupation.

All was hushed and effortless: flower-like girls, unreal and impersonal as show-window waxworks, waited upon us with smiles like confetti and low bows that seemed the caresses of a graceful humility. Down a shadowed stairway, muted with *tatami*, was the bath where, if need be, one of these silken maidens would vigorously scrub your back (they must surely be inviolate, these vestal creatures, so remote from all fleshliness did they appear); Kishi and I dispensed with this service, assisting each other's ablutions without the need of female help. In our room, before a bath, we would undress and put on the *kimono* provided by the hotel and the hotel slippers of plaited rush, silent and sybaritic, and descend to the bath where soap, brushes, towels and the rest were being laid out by one of the smiling maidens in whose mouth butter wouldn't melt, even at the sight of our nudity. It would be an indefensible breach of manners to use soap, or rinse it off, in the steaming, almost scalding, cauldron in which one did one's breathless soaking, immersed up to the neck, after soaping: all washing and sponging was done on the tiles and wooden gratings beside the bath proper—and that done, we sank together up to our chins and, gasping, watched the sweat beading upon each other's crimsoning visages.

In this manner one lived in Tokyo, staying in a very modest and small hotel: more luxuriously in some ways, and especially in the way of *feeling* luxurious, than in any Hilton-Astoria: too softly comfortable, perhaps, after a while—too indulgent and ornamental, as life was supposed to be, and probably wasn't, in ancient Sybaris—one came to feel one was eating too many sugary cakes. There was basically the same elegant comfort in Mama-San's upper rooms, but less yielding, less mellifluous; *tatami* covered the floor, and there was a pretty alcove for the ancestors; but the bare plastered walls seemed cold and austere. We moved, for a week or two, to a much grander hotel: though Japanese owned and managed, it was done in the European style—there were taps and running water and we slept, raised from the floor, on a bedstead—one hilariously frightening night we were tipped out with a bang on to the floor—whether the earthquake had caught us clasped together or whether sheer terror made us clutch each other, I can't say: but had we that night become corpses, we should have been found by our rescue party naked and locked in the closest embrace. How we laughed after that sharp little earthquake—and how frantic was my terror when, bumped into consciousness, there were still a few seconds of heart-stopping tremors to come.

And then we found our house, where we were to live for many more months to come: in some leafy outskirt of Tokyo, on a small hill, looking out at horizons embroidered in a multitude of greens; with the geometrical exactitude of Fuji-San, white-necked and pink-tipped, like an ethereal mine-tip, cast spectrally against the sky at dawn.

At neither of those hotels, where perfect manners were a part of the general excellence and urbanity, was the slightest hint of surprise shown when I, a foreigner, shared my room, and indeed my bed, with a fifteen-year-old boy. Nor did the elderly university professor who became our landlord and lived with his wife in the main wing of the house, show any surprise—and still less any displeasure; and retained, whenever I met him or called to pay the rent, the same smiling benignity of manner even after Kishi's cousins and friends had begun arriving in the mornings to cavort naked, like a line of animated sculptures, down the long colonnaded passage which connected our rooms with our bathroom (the house had an odd and ramifying layout). Our landlord was exactly like the caricature of a Japanese professor drawn by a cartoonist who didn't like Japan : smiling with a comic mask's teeth, and slit-eyes further hidden behind thick steel-rimmed spectacles; he always, indoors and out, wore a *kimono* with a Western trilby hat; in winter, for the street, he tied a black muslin veil over mouth and nostrils, to keep out the germs. But behind this illusion of sly shyness, there was plainly evident an acute and liberal mind and what one at once knew to be a wholly charming personality. Just what he taught, I didn't find out; his principal private interest, I discovered, was the study of vulcanology.

The house, in style, was neither Japanese nor European but attempted a synthesis of both. Our enormous room was stone walled, or of stuccoed brick, and had a couple of large European windows; but we lived "on the floor," on the exquisite civilization of *tatami*. The bathroom, too, was a kind of compromise between the Western and the Niponian : the tub itself was a huge European affair of unusual length and girth, while it stood in a large expanse of tile and duckboard for washing and rinsing *à la japonaise*. But the most delightful feature of our apartment was the dais which, like a Shakespearean stage, stood out from the long back wall and looked down on three sides upon a humbler level, as if it were built for the throne of a medieval king. On this our bedding was spread, while on the "ground floor" we ate and played and read and wrote—cross-legged on the *tatami*, and the typewriter on a foot-high lacquered table.

I was a newspaperman accredited to the American forces, and was consequently an "occupationnaire" (what eyesores of words get invented these days!)—a member, that is, of a highly privileged aristocracy. We were socially superior to all Japanese, including former prime ministers, admirals, members of the old House of Peers and so on : the humilities of defeat required from them to us an obeisance deeper even than ordinary good manners enjoined.

This aristocracy of conquerors gave us a great variety of

good things which the Japanese weren't allowed, like petrol and the hire of taxis and the best houses and hotels and entry to bars, cinemas and so on (a Japanese who owned an automobile, if he still owned it, had to cook himself a gas in a kind of kiln rigged behind the boot); a form of *apartheid* was the rule. We also—very valuable concessions these, and most useful to Kishi—were exempt from various taxes which the Japanese had to pay, and could buy things like cameras at about one-third the public price; and we had the run of the PX and later the British NAAFI—which between them sold everything almost one could think of, at wonderfully low cost. One of the laws of this *apartheid* was that severe penalties—expulsion from Japan, perhaps—awaited an "occupationnaire" who gave as a gift to a Japanese any "occupationnaire" goods : some privileged petrol, for instance, or anything bought at the PX.

So on a certain day of each week Kishi and I visited the PX, and on another day the British NAAFI (Kishi in the role of my porter); and we bought all the comestibles and household goods that Mama-San wanted (there was a great shortage at the time of things like sugar). And we bought too, clothes for Kishi and toys for the children—the family's delight over an electric train remains for ever vivid in my mind. On some of these expeditions, Kishi brought his cousin Suki : a simple stocky lad of Kishi's age, with a round, close-cropped head and a slight limp which gave him an individuality his features perhaps lacked. Then Suki, by invitation, found his way one Sunday morning to our house; and next week brought a friend of his and Kishi's; and each Sunday seemed to add another until a half-dozen boys would be arriving, bringing trays of delicacies and Japanese forms of "small chow" which Mama-San and other mothers had cooked specially; we'd have ready beer and orangeade, with cigarettes and sweets from the PX. The youngest of our visitors, I'd say, was thirteen; the eldest three years more : they were sweet-natured boys and full of fun; with lively minds and beautiful manners; skin like parchment and fiery black, interested eyes peeping narrowly from their deep settings. Only dear Suki was a bit dullminded; but none was sweeter-natured : it was he, always, who stoked the furnace for the bath, and he who looked after food and drink for everybody.

These mornings ran usually the same way. First, the bath; and then upon the splendid stage of our room, with the soft, springy, luxury of its *tatami* flooring, the play-acting and miming, the wrestling and gymnastical frolics, the romps and the fooling with the help of the Monkey Masks I'd brought from the island of Bali.

Suki would cram the old-fashioned iron stove with wood and light it; in no time the water in the tank over the bath would be bubbling hot, and the boys would be ready undressed in our room and jumping about excitedly. Then would come the dancing procession down the arcaded walk to the bathroom : a charming file of gyrating naked figures like a design on a Greek vase—which the Japanese professor, were he in the mood, could watch from his study-window. There followed the scene which, improving on *Three Men in a Boat,* I called "Six Boys in a Bath" : I wish I still possessed the photographs I took that provided such perfect illustrations of this theme : photographs of all six, splashed with soap-lather like badly whitewashed statues, or with their soapy hair twirled into horns or spirals or contorted and weird antennae; photographs of six pair of legs hanging from the knee down over the lip of the bath-tub, with six urchin faces grinning at knee-level; of a *mêlée* of wet limbs and fragments of anatomy, through a spray of splashing and thrashing water; of each in turn under the shower, caught in some fancifully contrived posture, while the rest queued up behind assuming naughtily comical attitudes; of vague incorporeal faces seen eerily in a haze of steam—I must have photographed them all in a score or two of posturings, groupings, and fanciful ablutionary occupations.

Bali is an island of dance; every child grows up a dancer, and there's a large tradition of dramatic ballet (much too snobbish and sophisticated a term for a form of expression as natural to the people as speaking) inbred in the people and born of their history. The Monkey Dance, in which fifty to a hundred men and boys take part, is one of the most exhilarating and spectacular of the whole repertoire. They wear masks, and when I came away from Bali after a month there early in 1950, I brought three of these masks with me. They're the masks of real monkeys, cured and mounted; perfectly fitting the average boy's face and transforming anybody, when the human eye from behind gives life and intelligence, into the semblance of a flesh-and-blood ape; a naked boy they transform into Pan or Silenus, into a humorous gargoyle of eighteenth century baroque, into god or devil or hobgoblin; into some fascinating if slightly nightmarish visitor from outer space. The effect of this bizarre hybrid is excitingly and extravagantly sexual—the hairy animal face seems to bring out all the eroticism of the glabrous naked body as sunlight brings out the richness of colours : even a Priapic effect, though without that deity's travesty of dimensions—one feels in the presence of an almost frightening virility.

There was a bit of squabbling over the masks but they all had a turn—three goblins at a time, and the others making faces in the wings with their own pliant features. Sometimes they'd be miming monkey habits : scratching under their armpits, searching each other's scalps; or they'd be wrestling on the soft *tatami* in a pantomime of the Japanese manner, an imbroglio of white contorted limbs and straining muscle; or their antics would become more stylised : they'd ape the formalism, perhaps, of old Japanese dance or the Noh theatre; or else, statuesque with sword or spear, they'd seem to be taking as their models old prints of the Samurai. Later in the morning, they'd sometimes be using another kind of Japanese print as a model (or so one might suppose) : those graphic portrayals of erotic exercises, conceived with superb ingenuity and exquisitely executed, for which Japan is famous. . . .

To the spectator, myself, all this was beautiful and disturbing : one had the impression of a breath-taking antithesis—Beauty and the Beast—between the white and touching innocence of these boys' bodies and the grotesque animality or fiendishness of their brutalized heads. It was like watching oleander buds blossoming into the likeness of Gorgons. I always felt that the boys of Japan, of Tokyo and the main island that is, seemed more tender, more fragile, than most other boys, in spite of their impishness and wiry strength; perhaps this feeling came from their dramatic contrariety : the purple-black heads of hair and raven eyes, against the almost death-like pallor of their skins and a glabrosity that wrenched at one's heart : even the oldest of these six hardly had a hair on his body.

*   *   *

The happiness I enjoyed in Tokyo was of a quality and volume so rare that when the break came, as it had to come, the pain seemed beyond bearing; but—a privilege that comes seldom in the peregrinant boy-lover's life—my friendship with Kishi continued into future years and even into Europe.

ROME

How THOSE delightfully outmoded Roman bathing establishments manage year after year to stand up against the tremendous weight of the Tiber's swift and muddy stream, bending and swirling for a dozen or more kilometres round its meandering banks of splendid masonry, I've never understood. I expect that nowadays most of the piles which support them are stone or concrete; but a lot of their patched-up timbers have to face the relentless power of this headlong river and bits of their upper-works must often get carried away during winter floods; yet summer after summer they awake from a pitiful hibernation and burst into rather squalid blossom with awnings and striped umbrellas and tatty little tables.

There must be some twenty of these *stabilimenti balneare* along the river between, say, St. Paul-without the Walls and the Ponte Milvio—the last city bridge to the north. They are interesting examples, even attractive in a "period" way, of what might be called nineteenth-century balnear architecture : vast wooden conglomerates of tiny dark cabins, as if hundreds of Victorian bathing machines had been welded into one piece. On their decks one feels oneself vaguely aboard ship or on the second-rate pier of some decaying English seaside resort. They might be a cross between the offspring of these two things and that of a college barge at Oxford and a village "longhouse" in Borneo.

Twenty years ago, on the Vatican side of the river and near the Ponte Sant'Angelo, there arose from the yellow stream the Stabilimento Barese (as I shall call it here), looking rather like some ancient pleasure craft on the Mississippi.

Six years later, I was disappointed to find, its character had entirely changed; but in 1948 Signor Barese's establishment was, during the summer's heat, the most attractive peg-house in Rome. It was a boys' brothel which fulfilled the most exacting demands of that term: the boys were there, and suitable accommodation was there and Signor Barese and his wife between them composed an obliging and friendly "madam." Food and drink were to be had at very reasonable prices, and there were spacious decks under the sun along which the boys in their little bathing briefs disposed their limbs charmingly.

The place was admirably cheap: the few cents of entrance-fee was within the reach of most Roman boys, and many who couldn't afford it waited on the shore opposite Signor Barese's establishment until somebody paid for them. A cabin for one's clothes cost, I think, a mere 100 lire (say a shilling), and one paid an extra 100 lire every time a visitor entered it. A very modest tariff.

And yet, although nearly all the boys and youths who dived and splashed from its platforms and who languidly displayed their slim forms on the sundecks, were willing, and many of them were anxious, to make a financial profit out of their afternoon's pleasure, nobody who didn't *know* would have guessed that the Stabilimento Barese was a male brothel; so unobtrusive were these heretical amours that those without eyes to see, like the bourgeois family parties and the bikini girls with attendant exhibitionist swains who came to the place in some numbers, seemed not to notice what was going on. I do, however, remember a certain lower deck—or was it at one end of the construction, well sunk between high bulwarks?—whose introductory flirtation was rather freer than in the more open decks; and where, some people might have thought, preliminary play before retiring to a cabin went a bit far. . . . And I remember Italo, a bronze-eyed boy with the oval face and neat features of the Old Roman—the stock, they say, breeds on in Trastevere, that ancient suburb caught in an elbow of the river south of the Vatican. Italo . . . he would be thirty-five years old now; married, no doubt, with half-a-dozen children. I hope so: he needed love.

I was away from Rome for six years; and I came back at the beginning of 1954. When the Tiber bathing establishments had put their coats of summer paint on and opened up their gangways in June, I made at once for Signor Barese's *stabilimento*. But his manner had changed completely: gone were his knowing nod, and his wife's prim amiability as she took the money for a visitor to one's cabin. Indeed, no visitor to one's cabin was allowed; an uninformed customer arriving with a boy companion and trying to hire a cabin for them both would be told curtly that he must take two cabins and that a watch would be kept to make sure that neither entered the other's. Signor Barese had taken to prowling about his decks on the lookout for any sign of lasciviousness between adult and adolescent: he behaved like a carpet-slippered housemaster patrolling the dorm at an English school. The boys still came there, deliciously inviting, to bathe and loll in the sun and—they hoped—be picked up: preferably by well-to-do foreign tourists. It was the "facilities" which had been withdrawn. "I don't allow *that* kind of conduct on *my* premises," Signor Barese would proclaim self-righteously; and the boys, if there were no better place to go, led their clients for a "stroll," a *passaggiata*, through the thickets of scrub and brushwood that spread like a canopy over the river-bank below the mausoleum of Hadrian.

I soon learned that some time during the years I was away there'd been a scandal; somebody had denounced poor Signor Barese for allowing boys of minor years to be led into immorality aboard his *stabilimento*. One could understand that thereafter—no doubt he was heavily fined, and was lucky not to see his establishment closed down—he was determined not to let it happen again; and by 1954 nobody could have been more diligent than Signor Barese in the preservation of adolescent virtue. To compensate for his loss of revenue to which this sort of propriety condemned him, he had raised the rental of a cabin from 100 to 300 lire.

When Signor Barese wasn't about, the boys, titillated by the sun and by the sight and feel of their own bodies, would amongst themselves indulge in those small comparative and competitive indecencies which are natural to boyhood all over the world. I remember especially Franchino, a leggy lad of fourteen whose interest in his own genitals seemed, whether he were alone or in company, to be unending; and a nice simple friend of his named Maurizio, whose curly auburn head reminded me of a dahlia. It was these two who first led me to the phantasmagoric world of fauns and satyrs that exists among the woodland and undergrowth running wild on certain reaches of Tiber's banks.

At the base of the immense walled embankments—the Tiber ploughs a dyke through the core of Rome thirty or forty feet below the level of the streets—runs on either side a shore as variegated in kind and configuration as the coasts of Calabria : here the walls drop to a mere tow-path; there, beyond a belt of tangled undergrowth spreads a gravelly beach; at another part, as between the Ponte Sant'Angelo and the Ponte Umberto, there's a wide ribbon of "jungle" in which boys can play all manner of games, invisibly to anybody who might be looking over the balustrade far above; or, again, the shore may rise steeply against the wall like the foothills of a mountain and be hidden by a coating of green tree and scrub and bracken and reed growing as thickly as any wild woodland. The whole Roman foreshore of the Tiber provides—or it did fifteen years ago—an enchanted jungle playground and an illusion of being a hundred miles from any city.

It became my playground too. Through the Spring I explored these banks from one end of Rome to the other; crept softly among the tangled bushes; glided under the silent trees; pushed a way through the waist-high scrub and fern. Down here, insulated from the sounds of the city by the immense height of these precipices of stone, there was, on a windless day, a strange, an almost haunted, hush : that sort of warm, odorous, pregnant quiet which, if one lets the fancy go, suggests to one's susceptible spirit the propinquity of Pan and his like; or, perhaps, of those delightful and libidinous and charmingly indecorous attendants upon Dionysus—of "Bacchus and all his crew." Indeed, in that glittering Latin sunshine and especially in the sweltering months of summer, one could quite often catch a glimpse, and more than a glimpse, through the lush foliage, of real live flesh-and-blood satyrs and juvenile sileni, with sweet urchin leers on their sallow Roman faces; warm, naked figures so like some marbles and bronzes of classic times that it seemed one could almost see the infant goat-horns growing from their skulls.

Swarms of boys swam from these banks, where swimming

cost them nothing and where, in the secret alcoves of the screening undergrowth after their swim—who cared what they got up to? . . . There were certain points specially suitable for bathing in this fiercely running river : places where a small stretch of beach made landing easy after a joyous drift down with the stream; one such was by the Ponte Umberto, under the Palace of Justice (a sylvan mound there was, where the boys undressed and hid their clothes : through the leaves, white naked flesh flashed and glinted like sunshine). But my favourite reach lay at the most northerly point of the city, a short way below the Ponte Milvio—a beautiful bridge still standing from classical times and famous as the spot where the Emperor Constantine, after seeing a vision of the Cross, won a great military victory.

At this bridge the city stopped. Above it, the river flowed through rustic fields; downstream, for half-a-kilometre or so, the banks between wall and water's edge were wide and ample and multiform as the Appenines in miniature : a low tree-covered tableland fell sharply to a belt of verdant prairie, from where a hard gravelly beach sloped gently to the water. It was a summer dreamland for the slum-boys of northern Rome : a landscape fraught with adventure and the requisites of pleasure—a field of entertainment of every sort far more attractive than the striped-umbrella-cum-jukebox "lido" provided at Ostia (Rome's seaside resort), and one which didn't cost a *soldo*. In the water or scampering on the beach, the boys wore trunks or underpants or a twist of rag—something to satisfy patrolling policemen watching from the bridge for breaches of the decency laws. But a bit inland, on the sandy clearings screened from unsympathetic eyes by thick high scrub or trellises of leaf, it was nobody's business what one did : here one could find rows of adolescent boys, naked as they were born, drying themselves in the sun or amusing themselves with the various stages of masturbation, from preface to postscript, which come as naturally after swimming to boys all the world over as chewing the cud does to ruminants after a good spell of grazing. I've often thought, indeed, that since masturbation is an important, and even needful derivative of adolescence, which should be made the best of rather than tabooed or lectured about, it should be initiated in the most natural and healthy circumstances possible : and where can these be better found than after a bathe : when the limbs, mildly tired, are pleasantly relaxing; the flesh is warm and deliciously enlivened by the sun, and the mind keenly aware of the sensations of nudity?

The Tiber is an earthy river, yellow and cloudy like some factory waste. It piles up above the Milvio bridge, one of whose two expansive arches is partially blocked, and then, squeezed between the pillars, races down in a great gush—faster, the stream looks, than a man can run. Bathing here isn't for babies or non-swimmers; even the strongest can only go in upstream and be carried down on to the beach some two hundred yards further down. It's fun, though risky more than a few yards from the water's edge. But there are plenty who risk it: flurries of boys dash down from the scrubby dunes and into the water, squealing and twittering like a cloud of starlings; others are baking on the gravel; and others again, in the sheltered privacies of the greenery above, are secretly engaged upon their private devices. . . .

*   *   *

I found Rome, through the year I lived there, a city where affection was hard to come by, though there was sexual blandishment round every corner. Human feeling, one fancied, had been soaked up by history and the architectural telling of it : there was none left for the hearts of simple people—one felt that love had been left out of Rome's platinum atmosphere. In none of the brief friendships I hoped I was making there did I find any desire for constancy; none lasted longer than the moment when the last extra hundred lire had been wheedled or blustered forth. Roman protestations of love, like gas-fires worked through a meter, go out unless the slot is constantly re-fed. Rome, I suppose, has always been a city of whores—writers under the Empire like Martial and Strato seem to make that clear; and John Addington Symonds, a perceptive and erudite English student of Greek and Roman eroticism, wrote in the last century : "Instead of love, lust was the deity of the boy-lover on the shores of Tiber." It still is. This long tradition of prostitution, and the honour of a classical prototype, perhaps exonerates the modern tourist (speaking generically) of a charge of corrupting the Roman boy-world; yet it is a truth of modern globetrotting society that where tourists abound (and their abundance everywhere is increasing at such a rate that before long, like the automobile to its owner, they'll become more a bane than a benefit to the countries who receive them) the boys quickly learn that they're the proprietors of a commodity which fetches a high price; and the market, of course, becomes irresistible. The foreign tourist, now that he's an industry and no longer merely a curiosity, has become a kind of chemical which starts corruption wherever he touches the native community that harbours him—the catering, hotel and retail trades, transport and so on; he manages to corrupt the art and architecture of a country by behaving like a football crowd when he visits the places his guidebook tells him he ought to see. And he even helps corrupt the national economy —governments apply huge sums of money, much needed elsewhere, to the "development" of tourism, this flood of foreign vulgarity which willy-nilly is becoming a deluge destroying the fields and vales of culture it engulfs.

To be fair to the tourist, one should say that his corruptive action is generally involuntary: it's the awareness of the money in his pocket that turns the decent citizens he comes amongst into cunning extortionists. But not always: his behaviour often corrupts by offending local taste: he gets drunk among an abstemious populace or affronts them with his unapt attire (would his wife, walking down Main Street at home, wear nothing but bikini and brassière?). There's a curious belief that the price of a tourist-ticket buys dispensation from the usual restraints of good manners. And in the sensual sphere his action is more deliberate still; here he doesn't merely passively leave temperance behind (the pronoun "he" stands for a considerable number of tourists)—he comes all out to get what pleasures he can't find in his home town, and convinced that his foreign currency will procure them. Of course he's right, generally; and his demand creates a supply.

It's the money that corrupts, not the sex: the money which combining with sex in a kind of psycho-chemical way, produces in the growing mind a condition in which sex becomes inseparable from money. Sex by itself is quite innocent. Money by itself, unfused with any of the agents in combination with which it generates power (and sex is one), is merely a useful thing to have. But money acting upon sex can destroy the capacity for happiness; it adulterates and sophisticates the emotions that make sex a principal vehicle of happiness, so that the mind that ought to be a young lover's becomes the equivalent of a shyster-shopkeeper's. Money, of course, plays a part in all human "love," in every sexual transaction however socially edifying : the purest young bride glances at her dowry or at least counts on being kept for life; the young lover feels impelled to take gifts to his beloved girl; a beloved boy looks for presents from his man lover. It's when money becomes more important than the sex, when the purpose of sex becomes money and the notion of the one evokes the image of the other that corruption of the emotions sets in. The guileless mind of the girl or boy becomes the calculating mind of the whore; and a principal source of happiness has been lost for good, before even it's been properly tasted. There can be no harm, surely, in linking a gift with any sexual transaction—corruption begins when the idea of "gift" turns into one of buying-and-selling and becomes a habit of mind.

The tourist rains down like some volatilized insecticide : encouraging, mainly among the semi-prosperous, patches of prosperity and, mainly among the unprosperous, a rush of cupidity to the head. He comes all the year round; but is at his thickest in August when better-off Romans are away : the poor remain, vulnerable to the tourists' toxic potencies.

So much for the tourist : rather pathetic, in spite of his aggressively carefree ebullience—a bundled-round child of the technological age (how our forbears on the Grand Tour would have shuddered at the idea of the "package tour"). He is with us for good : the day may come when nobody will stay at home and everybody will be "abroad." In the meantime, the demerits of "tourism," like those of automobiles-for-all, are rapidly outnumbering its benefits; one can only hope that both will bring about their own demise by, so to speak, swallowing their own tails.

Small wonder if there's a smouldering belief in Italy that tourists as a species are sexual marauders : people who regard Italy as an easy field for their erotic eccentricities. The pursuit of boys got the name in the eighteenth century of the *vizio inglese,* presumably because Englishmen on the Grand

Tour were more numerous than other European nationalities. Nowadays all Englishmen, Americans and Nordics generally are expected to go for the boys until they've shown that they don't want to. The reason for this is simple : boy-lovers from abroad are apt to arrive with two ideas in their heads—that all young Italians are to be had for the paying, and that it doesn't matter what you do because you're "abroad". In 1967 a southern Italian newspaper reported that two young Londoners were finishing their holiday in Poggireale prison in Naples—and waiting to be tried for committing *atti innominabili* with two adolescent boys in a rowing-boat which they'd hired at Mergellina. The "unnameable acts" were observed from the shore, police were told, and the boat-load was arrested while a "hostile crowd" gathered at the landing-stage. The lesson of this story lies in the touristic turn of mind it displays : the notion that in Naples it was all right to break several laws with two under-age boys in an open boat and on a stretch of water in full view of almost the whole Neapolitan seafront. At home, they know, they'd have been off their heads to behave so blatantly : abroad, and especially in Italy, anything goes.

*   *   *

But this corruption of boys by fusing in their minds the two notions of money and sensuality, so that thought of "cash" or "cockstand" automatically evoke each other, is an ancient Roman institution, not an importation of the tourist trade. Evidence unlimited of this may be found any evening or winter's afternoon in certain small cheap and shabby cinemas which tend to be tucked away in unobtrusive little back streets. I can remember three, especially, of these special little movie-theatres—specialized, one might call them—where men and boys crowded much more in order to perform the *atti innominabili* of which Petronius, Martial and Strato wrote than to watch some old tattered film; and where a constant game of musical chairs seemed to be played as men moved from one seat to another—from one boy to the next, like bees exhausting bloom after bloom—or the boys clattered about, seeking yet another likely client to sit beside. Generally the equivalent of three or four shillings changed hands after these cinema-seat skirmishes, according to the age and cunning of the boy. And never a tourist in sight.

They were very much "local" places of entertainment: one saw the same faces hungrily scrutinizing the probabilities of the audience while the lights were still up; and the boys who came there were mainly "neighbourhood" boys. In those days, nearly fifteen years ago, the prices were absurdly low—there was one, I recall, where one paid 40 lire (less than sixpence). On a cold winter's afternoon, then, or a day of unrelenting Roman rain, almost any boy could find enough money to get inside and, warmed by an accumulating concentration of human heat and reposing upon a shifting supply of wooden seats, pass a whole afternoon and evening with a flickering film to watch when he felt like it and, with luck, a few clients to provide cigarettes and cash. The knowing boy counted upon coming out better off than he went in.

One of the best-known of these places was the "Farnese," a small cinema in the Campo dei Fiori ("Field of Flowers"), a kaleidoscopic and picturesque market square set spaciously in the labyrinth of Old Rome; a street away stands Michael-angelo's prodigious and patrician Farnese Palace—the home nowadays of the French embassy—from which this cheeky little picture-palace impudently took its name. A ticket into the Farnese cost 80 lire which gave you the right to a seat, if you could find one, on the *platea,* or pit-stalls, or standing-room in the side-aisles which, for ogling perambulation and for feeling and fumbling far outran the old Empire Theatre promenade in Edwardian London.

Off one of the aisles there was a passage into an enormous pee-place as stately as any Farnese *salone* : here one's unheralded entrance might intrude upon all sorts of *atti innominabili.* But most of the activity took place in the auditorium—and even more so at another little cinema which I chanced upon one day and often visited during the first three months of 1954.

If this cinema had a name it wasn't displayed, and no neon lights decorated its dingy *façade*; only the posters outside, advertising strip-cartoon-heroics-type films, revealed that it was a cinema at all. The entrance was dark and poky and shabby, in a shabby and poky by-street off the Largo Argentina: that grandiose meeting-place of buses and trams (as it then was) on the main thoroughfare between Vatican and Piazza Venezia, and site of an excavation of antique masonry which, like other similar ruins, sheltered one of Rome's numerous herds of homeless cats—those strange feline colonies condoned by the municipality and nurtured by benevolent old women.

To get into this place, it cost at first only 40 lire—I remember being shocked later that winter by a rise to 50 lire. Its doors opened at two in the afternoon and by three o'clock it was packed : the early comers had grabbed the best strategical seats or made for likely looking persons to sit next to. Once the lights were down, the place seemed to become the landscape of some bizarre, half-lit dream—half lit by the hesitant luminosities of the screen, and half by the sensually illuminating discoveries of a hundred exploring hands. . . . One's seat chosen, one didn't know what might happen—though almost certainly something would. The boy beside one might casually take out his penis and work it into erection, with an air of its being the most ordinary thing to do in a public cinema; or he might wave it ostentatiously beneath one's nose, as if the thing were a challenge. Or, more restrained, the boy might merely open up his trousers and sit quietly waiting. Or else a boy of angelically demure aspect, his eyes fixed with apparent absorption upon the screen, wouldn't bat an eyelid of surprise or protest when one let fall a gentle inquiring finger on his lap. . . . The seat-backs, linked by strengthening battens, would frequently communicate to each other a rhythmic shuddering which would run down the row from one aisle to the other. After half an hour or so, the musical chairs would begin—people getting up and walking about looking for further prey; when the lights were turned up for interval and ice cream, everyone in the forward rows stood up and turned about, in order to see who and what were sitting behind. . . .

I was working most mornings and evenings—at that time I was writing articles for one or two London magazines—and in the winter afternoons there was little to do but go to a film. But since I'm not one to drop into any movie without first being assured it was a first-class one, and there being few of those, I was very often drawn to one of these *louche* places

I'm describing. . . . I went partly for the pleasurable titillation of the unknown, partly of course for the sensual excitement, partly for the thrill of "the hunt"—that thrill experienced by everybody on safari, even the most miniature sort; and partly too in that hope, seldom fulfilled in Rome, which every boy-lover nurses, of finding perfection—or something within range of it. But I went also for the sake of a perverse fascination which the cynicism of this wholesale sexual commerce had for me—everybody, I dare say, relishes being thrilled and shocked in one breath. I felt enthralled by the grotesque horror of these fumbling men (ignoring the fact that I was often one of them), and the venal obscenities of their cunning charmers; and by the wry comedy of the General Post and musical chairs that were constantly going on. I was appalled, and yet engrossed, by the proximity of so many cocks-for-sale; and by the pervasive diffusion of corruption-by-purchase. The air of the place seemed loaded with a vitalised eroticism that smelt of the water-closet and was the epitome of anti-love. Yet it captivated my imagination as, I suppose, the same atmosphere had captured Roman imaginations like Trimalchio's a couple of millennia ago. . . . One thing that should be noted is this : only a small percentage of the boys who make up the daily audiences in these cinemas would have called themselves prostitutes—would have agreed that, to use the London and Berlin expressions, they were "on the game" or *uff'n Strich*. They were mostly ordinary lower-class boys, at school or at work or looking for work; and, to them, what they did in the cinema was as ordinary a way of picking up a little pocket-money as running errands, and more pleasant. Yet the circumstances of their doing it implanted in their minds the notions that sex *was* prostitution, that what they had between their legs was a form of cash, like the Sunday suit at the pawnbroker's. . . .

I remember a third theatre which I visited a few times—in a narrow street running through from the via del Tritone to the Trevi Fountain, and thus bang in tourist country. Here entrance was more expensive; but there always seemed to be a boy or two on the lookout for a patron—a boy probably more consciously a "prostitute" than the youngsters in those other cinemas, since a number of avid tourists generally found their way here from the Trevi square, and mingled with the families of the Roman bourgeoisie. The game of musical chairs was played here with much greater discretion, and sexual behaviour was stealthy and governed by the utmost prudence. After all, quite a lot of people came in really wanting to watch the film. . . .

LONDON

A NOTICE painted on the well-weathered wooden palings says: "Men and Boys Only": welcome words to such as me, with their simple preclusion of that simpering sexual flaunting of the bikini classes which has become the chief business of "mixed bathing" establishments; and with their promise of artless and unpretending youthful nudity.

This bathing-place is on one of the green-and-golden lakes of Hampstead Heath: that's how I remember it in the summer of the 'thirties, when the yellow gravel banks were alight with sunshine and the water, deep and earthy-bottomed, was like lucent brown candy.

The vast breathing oasis of the Heath spreads out to the north of London behind the hilltop suburb of Hampstead, where the eggheads live, like a limitless evergreen switchback —a verdant expanse of classic parkland composed of knoll and hillock, dell, woodland and lake and rippling pasture or lawn of springing turf. It is the Londoners' most beautiful refuge from reality; but, being given over to public enjoyment, its beauty is spoiled by the public's enjoyment of it. Where once Keats listened to the nightingale, one now hears the public's automobiles; and where all should be solitude and whispered intimacies of rusticity, the seeker after sylvan seclusion will today find it only at about 7 a.m.—but even then he will probably encounter a number of earnest eggheads striding healthily through the morning air.

But at the bathing-place, on the contrary, the lyric beauty of the surroundings, for me at any rate, is enriched by the flesh-and-blood beauty of its public: a public, more than half of it, of bathing boys big and small—the water is too deep for non-swimming infants; and, since there is no entrance money to be paid, boys of all classes flock there on hot summer days: the poorest from the North London slums or the posh-voiced sons of the Hampstead eggheads. One can hear every inflection of London's marvellously graduated speech; from the suave superior vowels of the BBC-middle class—"Oh, Rupert, do hurry up and come in: the water's absolutely super," the idiom as well as accent, alien to the cockney—to, now and then, the rhyming slang of the juvenile near-underworld. "Wasser matter, mate," I once heard a youngster say to another, "ain'tcher comin' in off the topboard wiv us?" "Don't feel like it," said the other, "I'm tired." "Tired?" exclaimed the first. "You bin pullin' yer 'ampton?"

It didn't take long to translate that. " 'Ampton" plainly stands for "Hampton," and Hampton Wick is a small town near London: "wick" rhymes with "prick." This was the first time I'd heard that phrase; "pulling your pudding" is an old and widespread figure of speech, but nowadays the almost universal term for masturbation among the working-classes is "wank": a word with a respectable long English history properly spelt "whank." Higher up the social ladder the vocabulary has euphemisms like "rub off," "rub up," "frig" and of course "toss off." I doubt whether "wank" has yet reached the public schools. English colloquialisms for "penis" also are apt to betoken the social level of their users. "Prick" might be called basic English: as old as the hills and used generally by the lower classes; "cock" and "dick" prevail through two or three layers of gentility upwards, and "thing," with an honourable literary and social past, is still found among the lower boys of some public schools; "old man," "weapon" and "tool" are all middle and upper class, the first two preferred by the heartier types like stockbrokers or in Army messes, while "tool" has something of an academic ring. In such a presbytery of the proprieties as the Athenaeum Club the penis would probably be referred to, if it were referred to at all, as "John Thomas" or, more discreetly, "J.T." (the first use of this euphemism noted by Eric Partridge's *Dictionary of Slang* occurred about 1840).

Another pleasant bit of rhyming slang I heard in the sun-bathing enclosure here was "Kick 'im up 'is 'arris"—said

by one boy advising another what to do to a third. " 'Arris"
was how I saw it in my mind—I felt that there must be a
dropped *h*; but I was wrong. The solution, when I got it
much later, was as charming as Euclid : "Aris"="Aristotle"
which rhymes with "bottle"; "bottle"="bottle-and-glass"
which rhymes with "arse." Q.E.D.

These British boys' physiognomies are as variegated as their
accents; their faces spell the alphabet of the English ancestry
which at its richest is as eclectic as the English language and
at its poorest as stodgy as English cooking : no other nation,
perhaps, shows such a marvellous diversity of physical styles.
The "average" British boy, if there be one, has a homelier
face than the fairy-tale Nordic type and has rarely the classic
look of the South European; he's a mousy sort : apple-cheeked
around puberty, and, like most fair-skinned boys—and girls
for that matter—shows through adolescence that peculiar
lustre which darker skins conceal. At his best he has the
cheerful snub good looks of the illustrations to school-stories.
But the British boy is very apt to run to nose; and at this
bathing place, where in the sun-bathing enclosure nakedness
is natural, there is plenty of chance to test the old theory that
a long konk bespeaks a long cock (a theory that I have found
is as often proved right as wrong). A great many boys in
England, in fact, are ugly; one sees more plain faces than
pretty or good-looking or handsome ones—France alone, I'd
say, in Europe, has more ugly boys than England. Plainness,
however, and even downright ugliness, is not the same thing
as unattractiveness; charm, even sexual, is far from always a
matter of feature or profile : charm is the impalpable radiance
of an expression—the sweetness or puckishness of a smile, the
spirit in the depths of the eye, the delights of a voice; charm, as
we all know, can transmute the apparently unlovely into
beauty; and human ugliness, so used to being slighted, can be
exciting : "I *like* them ugly," Stuart Mason, the great biblio-
grapher of Oscar Wilde, used to declare half a century ago.
"They get so little opportunity. . . ."

*   *   *

It was a Thursday afternoon that I first saw Neddy and
Ted, lying together limp and bemused by the sun; drops of
water, left from their bathe and still unevaporated, glinted on

their bare white skins like tiny bubbles of light. Thursday was early-closing day for shops in North London; and Neddy and Ted, I learned later, were both errand-boys in Hampstead: one for a greengrocer's, the other for a provision-store—they rode those cumbrous delivery bicycles which, once an engaging commonplace of London's streets, have now been ousted from traffic by the supermarket along with the other pleasant familiarities of the round-the-corner shop. Today there are few errand-boys.

Both were fourteen; they lived in the same street and had gone through school together; both were named Edward but never so called. Now they worked in shops in the same block, and after work wherever one went the other went too; they called for each other after they'd had their teas as naturally as they woke up in the morning. They were "mates" and knew each other's minds and bodies as well as they knew their own. When a London boy refers to another as "me mate," he's admitting to an intensity of loyalty and alliance he'd be shocked to think of in such "wet" terms. Neddy and Ted would have called anybody a cunt who told them they loved each other.

They were lying stretched on their backs, with their heads a few inches from my toes; so that I looked down on trickling hair and the arcs of eyelids closed against the sun, and the taut dome of ribs diving to the flats of stomachs. I could watch the clockwork of their hearts and the secure motion of their breathing. They were voluptuously unmoving on the hot concrete floor; absorbing the tingle of the sun with all the vehemence their skins were capable of—the delicious opposite of the sting of their first dip. Their wet swimming trunks were beside them in small dark slimy heaps, like bits out of the washtub. They'd dropped their towels across their middles—a *douceur,* one might call it, to Jack the Keeper who, executor of the decency laws, fitfully appeared among the sunbathers to grumble to any whose nakedness wasn't even symbolically hidden: "Cover y'self up." One of the boys, the smaller and fairer, had tucked his towel under him and brought up between his legs a figleaf triangle—from the hypotenuse of which impudently poked a sprinkle of rust-red hair. His body had the skimmed-milk look of the very fair at the beginning of the bathing season: skin translucent almost, and painfully fragile—one felt one could see the bones beneath. His mate, who was bulkier and dark-haired, had skin faintly mottled, like milk that's been standing in the dust.

"Neddy," he said suddenly, "I wish we 'ad a fag. It wouldn't 'alf be smashing then." ("We," he had said, not "I": the fag, if there were one, would be shared.) This of course was my opportunity: I had merely to pull out my cigarettes, and the way would be open. . . . But somehow I didn't; I was happily bemused by the beauty of these two supine boy bodies, so touchingly unconscious of their beauty; by the sylvan peace of the trees overhead and the brilliance of the sky; by the dazzle and dapple on the concrete of this precocious summer in May. I was quite happy simply looking at these two boys—I felt I couldn't look at them long enough. Later, I thought to myself, later . . . there's plenty of time. . . .

It was early in May, and a weekday; the place wasn't crowded and was pleasantly quiet, as if it were engrossed in its own thoughts. Apart from the background shouting and splashing from the lake outside, which one felt rather than heard, the only sounds came from opposite corners of the enclosure, occupied as usual by pietists of two rather incompatible heliolatrous sects: the eggheads and the weight-lifters. The eggheads were a bony, bearded group of spindly men who, for the most part, sat in cramped and ossified postures like those of the mummies of Pompei: altering these attitudes every ten minutes or so in order to expose a fresh segment of their flesh to the sun: while they murmured together (at the time of which I'm writing) of Pound or the Woolfs or Auden or the Spanish war, and chuckled discreetly over their little intellectual jokes. The eggheads kept to themselves and harmed nobody. The weightlifters and their allies the boxers, mostly retired, were rather different: they were an extroverted lot of men who liked to have an audience. If one didn't watch their feats of strength of one's own accord, they glared challengingly—almost menacingly; one kept one's freedom only by avoiding their eye. They spoke in a kind of movie-dialect of cockney-American; and manifested their prodigious muscles while hissing loudly through their noses. They kept in their corner a boxful of weightlifting equipment; and there was a good deal of clanking and gasping as they hoisted up and down huge lumps of lead or iron bars. The weightlifters' obsession with muscular enlargement didn't seem to be a matter of rivalry; they'd no desire, as far as I could see, to grow bigger biceps than the others or lift heavier lumps. It was their own muscles, their own bodies, they were interested in and nobody else's : they contemplated their own limbs and watched their own flesh with the absorbed attention that a woman gives to her face in the looking-glass. I don't know what the psychologists say about the body-builders and muscle-fetishists; I feel they have a corner in an exclusive sort of kinkiness : aggressively extrovert in manner, they are yet turned in on themselves, fascinated by their own proportions, bewitched by a kind of butch narcissism. They may believe that women fall for this mighty muscularity; I can't help thinking, though, that the body-builders may be terrific masturbators before the mirror.

The other sunbathers were solitary and unobtrusive; there were, of course, one or two queers : one can always tell them by following their eyes. Schoolboys clattered in from outside in ones and twos or a flurry of half a dozen, tore their clothes off and rushed out to the water, and rushed back like a cloud of dripping sparrows, pulling off their wet trunks and gyrating their arms like flails, in the way boys have, to dry themselves, and all shouting at once.

"'Oo's comin' in again?—ain't 'alf good! . ..."

"Like bleedin' ice, it is. . . ."

"Lets 'ave a dry on your towel, Jim. . . ."

"Blimey Bill, your bollocks is shrivelled up like a bit of cold tripe. . . ."

"Look at Bill's knackers—like a bit o' cold tripe. . . ."

"Oo's got any fags? . . ."

"I'll sell you a dog-end for a penny. . . ."

*　　　*　　　*

The gentle murmur of the eggheads seemed as mellow as the humming of bees and, through the haze of my enjoyment, the clank-clank of the weightlifters came vaguely like the remote shunting of trains in a happy night. The sun had dried the two boys' heads now, and I realized with a silly little excitement (why is it that the unusual often has charm for its own sake?) that the smaller one's hair was coloured a shade of freckled auburn—a red roan one might call it, throwing off sparks where the sun hit it: beneath this fiery crown were the cheeky yet touching features of a bronze satyr in a Sicilian museum—or, for that matter, a flesh-and-blood satyr in any Sicilian street: a delightful face, pale of course instead of swarthy, that was at once rueful and decadent and impish. The eyes, I found later, were pale brown with streaks of gold.

Suddenly he turned his head sideways to the other. "Ted," I heard him whisper. "Oy Ted, wake up. I got the 'orn." And sure enough, when I looked, I saw that the triangle of towel had become a bivouac tent. Then he reached down and bunched the towel in a heap over his privates. "Oy, Ted, d'you 'ear? What about it?"

Ted's eyes opened but he didn't answer; he seemed to be pondering over Neddy's remark. After a minute he muttered; "Now you got me started"; and it was his turn to pile his towel into a prudent heap. There was a brief whispering— and in a moment I knew what it was about.

With one mind they stood up, clenching their towels astutely round their telltale bodies; and made for the door that led to the lake. I knew they would turn right, and follow the concrete path among the lakeside trees to a small copse that stood by itself and contained the structure labelled "gents"— a primitive yard with a gutter at the base of the wall and two wooden cubicles that could be bolted from the inside. I gave them a couple of minutes and then quietly followed.

As I expected, they were in one of the cubicles together, with the door bolted. Creeping barefoot on the concrete, I shut myself silently in the other. Through a crack in the boarding I knew perfectly well a thread of daylight ran down the partition: a tiny crack which in two or three tactically chosen spots had been widened with the point of a penknife— by earlier generations, I suppose, of dirty old men. Peeping one-eyed through these spyholes, I could watch just what Neddy and Ted were doing. . . . The whole of the little edifice seemed to be gently oscillating like the housing of a small marine engine; there was a regular thump as Neddy's knuckles softly hit Ted's belly, and a rhythmic creaking from the lavatory seat. The muscles of Ted's thighs, toes and feet, stretched stiff into the air, were vibrating with a kind of tremor; his mouth was slightly open, and his eyes seemed to be watching without seeing the dust dancing in a streak of sunlight. I could see both their faces clearly by looking up slantwise through the crack. There was a look of screwed-up petulance in Neddy's expression, as if he were finding his work unrewarding. "Turn it in, Ted," I heard him whisper. "Do yer own, can't you? I want me own bleedin' wank." . . . Then I lost count of detail. I can remember a general consciousness of vibration, of beat and rhythm and a mounting sense of infatuation; I seemed to become blinkered from real things in a dementia of wanting to *see* all of these two boys all at once; their entranced and swooning eyes, their mouths hot and quick-breathing, the movement of their hands and the responding phallic shapes and angles and shades of colour: I yearned to feel with them through their fingers, through every sensory nerve and tissue they possessed, the same feelings that they were feeling. . . .

* * *

Why, I ask myself, why should this spectacle, this peepshow, or any like it, give me through my eyes a pleasure more intense than any other I can think of? Why should the secret witnessing of one or two boys masturbating bring mental and emotional sensations of a quality drawn otherwise only from aesthetic experience? Why, why? It seems so silly. This strange pleasure isn't just the voyeur's prurient enjoyment, the mere satisfying of one's natural sexual interest; sexual it is, of course—yet it is a pleasure of the spirit: the fierce, rarefied joy that surges through one's being from the words of a writer of genius. It's the pleasure one feels in the presence of *beauty*. But why it should be so, I can't explain. That word "secret," perhaps—"the *secret* witnessing"—may contain a clue to part of the mystery: a boy entranced by approaching orgasm, believing himself alone and absolutely secure from others' eyes, drops all pretence and defence from his expression; he is for these few moments utterly free of those unconscious inhibitions which through his waking life mask his face and eyes, always on the defensive: the secret watcher, the Peeping Tom if you like, catching the boy thus with his guard off, feels that he's looking into the boy's mind and heart and soul—that he's somehow joined to him in an unattainable intimacy of the spirit.

* * *

We came out of the cubicles at the same moment; from the way they looked at me I knew they were wondering what I had heard or guessed—they couldn't know that I'd *seen*. . . . Ted started whistling loudly, and Neddy said, a little self-consciously : "We going to the pictures tonight, Ted? There's a good one up at the Regent. . . ?" "I ain't got no money," Ted answered.

Back in the enclosure, they began to dress in a dawdling way : their clothes on the long bench round the palings were only a yard or two from mine. They went on talking about the pictures; and then started whispering together, and throwing glances now and then at me.

"I would for a shilling," I heard Neddy say. A shilling! A pathetic little sum : the average "present" expected thirty or forty years ago by a London boy who more for fun than anything was willing to join you in a bit of sex, was half-a-crown—" 'alf-a-dollar" they called it. (You could get a movie-seat, then, for ninepence and cigarettes cost sixpence for ten.)

I took them into Hampstead for a tea of eggs-an'-chips and creamy cakes; and gave them more than enough money for the film. Next Thursday, which would be their half-day again, they would come to my flat for tea—and, they told me, "games".

After that, for several months, they came every Thursday; and our routine was always the same. My bath was a big one, with both width and depth; and as soon as they came, I had to fill it with steaming hot water : so deep that when they both were in, the water almost swilled over the edges. They'd have their clothes off in no time : then for the next hour or so they would lie and wallow and giggle and squeal, while their bodies turned the colour of cooked lobster and they "swam" and "played submarines"—submerging all of their bodies except their floppy wet "periscopes"—or amused themselves with small obscene pranks and the demonstration and comparison of each other's bodies. When they'd had enough of this, and were drying their steaming skins, I would be getting their tea ready. It was always the same : scrambled eggs on toast—three eggs each—followed by chocolate éclairs. This they always ate with no clothes on at all : it was one of the rules they had laid down themselves. I can remember so well the pattern that the cane-seats of the chairs impressed upon their soft scarlet bums; and Neddy's small bony arms sawing away at his scrambled eggs on toast.

When the first cigarettes after tea had been smoked half-way to the end, I knew exactly what would come next. Neddy's little cheeky face would look up at me and he'd throw me his impish grin. "Hey, Ted," he'd say, "let's git up on the bed. Mick's going to give us our luvverly feelings—ain't you, Mick?" This was always the name of the third act of our Thursday entertainment—the Luvverly Feelings; the first two being the Bath and the Scrambled Eggs. Neddy would stretch out on his back on one side of the big bed, his white, delicate limbs, relaxed and limp, looking touchingly fragile and his arms spread out expectantly like the arms of a crucifix; the hollows of his glabrous armpits were like small cups of marble. Ted's place was along the other edge of the bed; and from my position between them I would administer the luvverly feelings : with the tips of my fingers I would stroke and titillate and fondle every part of their bodies, moving downwards from their arms and breasts and over their bellies, or upwards along their thighs, until my hands reached the topmost fringe of their pubic hair or the supine silky folds of their scrotums : then my fingers, moving with the gossamer delicacy which the boys—and especially Neddy —had insisted they should attain would explore all those secret nooks of the flesh and areas of exquisite sensation which are lumped together under the shamefaced official cover of "private parts." And so the luvverly feelings came to the inevitable entrancement of their end. The boys were always delightfully happy and natural after the luvverly feelings. They were uncomplicated boys; though they were united by the immense affection that each felt for the other, and though from infancy they had grown up together into sexual knowledge and action, they showed no sign of the slightest deviation from the emotionally normal—there was nothing queer about them. They healthily regarded their bodies as a means of getting amusement and pleasure of a kind which they didn't in their minds connect with shame or guilt; when they felt like doing something sexual, they did it—as naturally as they ate when they were hungry. The wanking experiments they had performed together; their first girls whom, they would boastfully announce each week, they were going to have at any moment now; even the unconventional innovations of our luvverly feelings—all, in their view, were part of a special segment of life which brought them enjoyment all along the scale from fun to their whole being's bliss. They couldn't see anything "dirty" about it.

As the weeks went by, they began to talk of bringing their "bits of skirt," when they'd found them, to my place; and they'd loudly gloat over the things they would do to the girls. "Just you wait, Mick," Neddy would say with his impish satyric grin. "You just watch me tell me bird to Get Up Them Stairs!" Or Neddy would say: "Eh Ted: when we gets our birds up 'ere, Mick 'll give 'is luvverly feeling to all four of us—won't you Mick?" "No, 'e won't," Ted would reply firmly. "I'm going to give me own bird me own luvverly feelings."

Some three months after these Thursday entertainments began the boys announced that they'd picked up a couple of girls outside a Hampstead cinema, and could they bring them to tea the following Thursday? I answered: "Of course." Though I realised this meant running an even greater risk than usual, I didn't want to snub them or to hinder the natural development of their emotional lives— and I thought I could probably prevent things reaching a dangerous point. For the rest of that afternoon they were boasting of the things they'd do next week when the girls were there. "Oh boy! Once I get me bird flat on that bed, . . ."—and Neddy finished the sentence with a bewitchingly wicked leer.

Next week I got in extra eggs and éclairs; though until the last minute I didn't believe any girls would come. But punctually to the minute Neddy and Ted arrived, blushingly ushering two plump and shiny girls, giggling and simpering, called Glad and Doreen. They were shy, gauche girls, smelling rather unpleasantly of cheap scent, but they had nice manners and were obviously determined to behave like perfect ladies.

But the boys' behaviour was even more demure: not a word or gesture that wasn't strictly party-manners; and the four of them spent the time playing ludo. Shortly after this I began to see less and less of them, as their entry into the world of girls took them wider afield. The interlude of the luvverly feelings was over.

BALI

RECENTLY I read a paragraph in the London *Times* headed: "Bali As a World Tourist Resort." The message came from Singapore:

Singapore and Indonesia are to collaborate to develop Bali as an international tourist resort, Dr. Goh Keng Swee, the Finance Minister, has disclosed . . . he and his Indonesian counterpart, Dr. Frans Seda, had recently discussed the project in Manila with some American financial interests. . . .

This is the *coup de grâce*: it will complete the extinction, begun nearly twenty years ago by the Javanese politicians, of the world's last island of innocence.

Until about 1950 the inhabitants of Bali, a minute segment of the Indonesian archipelago and a tiny dot of easygoing Hinduism on a map of Islamic ambition, was as innocent of worldly corruption as, to use an analogy of the English ironist Samuel Butler, a newlaid egg: they weren't interested in money; they didn't care about conventions, except the comfortable conventions of politeness which make human relationships graceful; they weren't embarrassed by the human body; they didn't believe that life should be a succession of duties to the community, or the state, or the nation, or the fatherland (though there were kindnesses that one naturally performed for one's neighbours and one's village and household gods); it had never occurred to them that work was virtuous in itself or anything other than getting something done that needed to be done; they had never supposed that the soil that grew them rice, the sea that brought them fish, and the trees that bore them coconuts and fruit could be made to provide the chemical or mineral ingredients of destruction—or that the many sorts of creature like caterpillars and grasshoppers which made dainty garnishes for their rice ought to be annihilated with insecticide; they had never for a second suspected that American financiers could see in their beautiful, simple and happy-go-lucky island a source of profit on investment capital; and they prized everyday, ordinary, morning-to-night enjoyment for man, woman and child, above anything else they could think of.

But soon after the Javanese nationalists had got rid of Dutch colonial rule; soon after the inevitable political arrogance which, alas, always follows the achievement of a new nationhood, had gone to the heads of the Muslim government of the new and sovereign Indonesia (such a strangely unimaginative "European" name for this unique and seductive agglomeration of polygenous Asian peoples); soon after the managers of revolutionary power in Jakarta (as Batavia had become) had found time to look around for centres of individualism where they could suitably interfere with people's lives and decree their conformity with the new order—soon after all this the attention of Java's revolutionary reformers turned to Bali.

This was an island of infidels—and revolutionary Java was Islamic; it was an island where, since memory began, women as well as men went bare-breasted and would have thought it improper if they didn't—and the Javanese revolutionaries were imposing the usual outward signs of revolutionary puritanism; the people of Bali were a gentle, peaceful, fun-loving lot who hadn't bothered much about the revolution and were even rather fond of the Dutch—gentleness, passivity and a desire to mind one's own playful business couldn't in these stirring times be tolerated. The Balinese even rather liked their old-fashioned modes of aristocratic government: there were five tiny toy kingdoms each under its own rajah, and every village had its own prince—and they were content with the fairy-tale system their island had been accustomed to since, they supposed, the beginning of time. So the Javanese missioners moved in—Muslim or Communist and anyway puritanical reformist—and the first thing they did was to order that female breasts should be covered up: the wearing of blouse or shift became obligatory, a measure in the interests of public morals which naturally was welcomed by the drapers of Jakarta and Surabaya. All kinds of reforms were introduced, and gradually the old aristocratic pattern was replaced by the rule of bureaucracy. (Under the old system, I don't think anybody was plebeian: there were merely higher ranks of nobility than one's own.)

In view of this Javanese sacrilege, of this alien eroding of the age-old Balinese ways of life and belief, I wasn't surprised when I heard, some years ago, of the volcanic catastrophe which destroyed so many of those lovely villages and paddyfields and coconut groves—and necessarily, too, alas, alas, so many of those beautiful and pure-spirited people, among them some, I fear, who'd been my friends. I wasn't surprised because these people's belief in their all-powerful gods who lived on the summit of the great mountain, the Gunung Agung—the very volcano that erupted—was so intense and *real* that obviously these gods wouldn't just watch all this sacrilege going on and do nothing about it; and the handiest vehicle for the utterance of their rage and the wreaking, possibly, of a bit of vengeance, was their own mountain which they could loose off without stepping off it. To us, who don't deal with gods of this kind, it seems an odd brand of vengeance—the demolition of their own domain and devotees. But the gods, especially when angry, have always been notoriously perverse.

This bungled demonstration of divine wrath, giving a fortuitous fillip to the political intrusions from Java, caused a further profanation of the innocence of Bali—a much-publicized spectacular disaster always brings a horde of bureaucrats, and the appearance of refugees attracts reformers and doctrinaires from all quarters. And, doubtless, thousands of these sweet and guileless islanders, driven by their own gods from the soil that had always seemed part of their own flesh, must have migrated to the sophistications of their worldly Javanese neighbour.

And now comes the third blow, and this time a mortal one from which there's no survival—"American financial interests." I remember, twenty years ago, the arrival of a fellow-guest at the admirable—almost luxurious for those parts of that epoch—hotel in Denpasar, the "capital" of the island: one of those American lady globetrotters whom one has encountered for decades all over Europe and, more recently I suppose, here and there in the Far East. She had arrived by air, as one did even in those far-off days, from Surabaya, and settled into the best room at the Denpasar Hotel. But next morning she left by the first aircraft, flying back to Java without seeing anything of Bali—she could not possibly, she explained while paying her bill, stay in any place where iced water wasn't provided by her bedside. Well, when Bali becomes a "world tourist resort" there will be plenty of iced water, and of everything else that Americans or any other tourists want. But there will no longer be Bali.

I had the good fortune to know Bali before any of these blows fell—only the Javanese blow was threatening to fall; I paid three visits to that blessed island staying for up to a month or six weeks at a time. "Good fortune" is a travesty of what I meant to say: some hyperbole like "unique privilege" or "priceless gift" is what's wanted: for Bali in those days was like the Garden of Eden before the Fall, if by Fall one means man's absorption into the worldly stream of money-grubbing, place-hunting, snobbery and vulgarity which happened the moment he became *homo economicus*. Bali was then paradise: not only, materially, because of the lavish generosity of its soil and verdure—one could almost live by picking things off trees from where one sat; not only, scenically, because its volcanic structure and tropical luxuriance made it, with its coasts and mountains, as beautiful an island as any existing; not only, aesthetically, because nine of its inhabitants out of ten, male and female, were artists of one kind or another, to whom craftsmanship or creativeness came as naturally as growing up; not only, emotionally, because the mood of the island seemed continually to be one of happiness and pleasure; but also, humanly, because the people of the island were innocent—innocent of the sins of monetary materialism. In fact, the native of Bali hadn't then become a proper *homo economicus*: true, people owned property, there were rich and poor, capitalists and wage-earners (though no industrialists)—yet the ordinary people weren't interested in money; if a person performed a service, he didn't ask to be paid in cash but was grateful for some small gift—a new sarong, perhaps, or—what had become very smart in the town—a European-style shirt.

In order to convey—before relating one or two personal tales of Balinese friendship—my own impressions of the island, I don't think I can do better than quote what I have written elsewhere :

". . . a green and flowering mountain rising rampant from the sea, with skirts of feathery palm and a violent volcanic crown; a fragment of verdant paradise between the eastern tip of Java and the island of Lombok . . . it's the sort of island where, when you're thirsty, a boy swarms like a monkey up a palm trunk and knocks you down a coconut.

"I think a Greek island in the bloom of Pericles' time may have been a little like it : an island of aristocrats whose life of pleasure and flourishing art was supported by slavery —the slavery, on Bali, being provided by the generous earth. One did enough work in the padi fields to harvest rice enough to satisfy one's belly and the Rice Goddess, the Rice Mother; for the rest of the time one was happy : one danced (so many dances, theatrical or ritual, perfectly performed by exquisite little girls or handsome, epicene youths); or one painted delicate pictures of monkey-like people stooping over the padi and human-like monkeys playing among the palms; or listened to tremendous Brandenburgian concerti played by an orchestra of gongs thirty musicians strong; or carved strange goblin figures in wood; or chiselled the easy soft stone into temples worthy of the gods; or fashioned head-dresses like mitres, like Cleopatra's tiara, out of the blooms of jasmine; or one squatted under a banyan tree making much of one's fighting-cocks or playing with one's crickets captive on a thread. One drank, stronger than coconut milk, the delicious 'beer' called tuak, brewed from the sugar-palm; and ate with one's rice, off palm-leaf plates, pork or chicken, dragon-flies, flying ants and the larvae of bees; and one went down to the golden sands, palm-fringed, where the catamarans were beached, and bathed in the gay breakers, not swimming out because of the killer barracuda and vaguely covering one's genitals with a fluttering hand for convention's sake (as the mouth is covered when yawning). One wore the soft flowing simplicity of the sarong; and one chatted cosily with one's village Prince, careful only to sit on a lower level than his, and to address him in his superior upper-class language while he spoke to oneself in one's baser, lower-class language (five tongues, I think, were spoken, including Brahmini Sanscrit and excluding Dutch) and one gazed, if one were a barbarian from industrial civilization, in humble wonder at this sweet and gentle human happiness, set against the torrential greens of padi and palm : a happiness that sprang from beauty and the spontaneous creation of beauty. Everyone was an artist from infancy; they were people of the *mind,* as well as of the body. . . ."

On one of my visits to the island I stayed in the village of Saba as guest of its Anuk Agung, or "prince" as foreigners rendered that august title : "agung"—as in Gunung Agung, the name of the mountain which is the home of the gods— means "great," "mighty," "illustrious" : a combination of all three. Saba was a large village in the verdant foothills of the mountain and a mile or so from the seashore. A stone wall, like a miniature fortification, ran right round the village, entered through ornate gateways in the Indo-Chinese style. Each household had its own pavilion, spaciously separate from its neighbours and built of the soft, red-brown stone which the village's masons and sculptors so skilfully fashioned into gargoyles and arabesques and moulded ornamentation— everybody's home was more like a pagoda than a mere house. And each home had its own walled courtyard, in which stood a small stone temple like a dovecot in which the gods lived : the god's chamber appears to be quite empty, for they are astral beings without visible substance. The village, like every village on Bali, had its own *gamelan*—full orchestra of gongs, xylophones and tintinnabula which together, played by true musicians, produced a glorious torrent of melody, having the tempo and zest as I've hinted above, of Bach at his most spirited; and, of course, its own company of dancers, girls and boys; and its own woodcarvers, painters and sculptors of stone.

The grandest pavilion was the Prince's; ornamented in what might be called oriental rococo and with a wide loggia reached by flights of steps on three sides—toy versions, one might say, of those majestic stairways which climb up to Santa Maria Maggiore in Rome. Me, the Anuk Agung had installed in a small dwelling not far from his : one room, a luxurious loft, on the upper floor, supported by a pillared arcade below and gained by a ladder. I looked out on to the special walled enclosure in which the *gamelan* performed its nightly rehearsals—fortunately I loved the tempestuous gusto as well as the intricate melodies of these massed percussive batteries; especially when comfortably mellowed by *tuak* and particularly when these enjoyments were shared with a brown-skinned young vassal of my princely host.

On my first evening, during that exquisite half hour when the dragonflies are still darting in the final glitter and when time seems to be waiting for that sudden eclipse of daylight which is the tropical sundown, I was sitting on the lower steps leading up to the Prince's terrace—he himself, of course, sitting above me on the top step. A number of his subjects— householders and retainers and a crowd of boys of all sizes eager to gape at the foreign visitor—were gathered on the steps about us, each of course placed according to his rank and all lower than the Prince. (There was one man, fortunately, who had been to school in Java and who understood enough English to interpret.) They all wore the sarong and most were barefoot; a very few wore a shirt or singlet and many of the boys had a rose or a sprig of jasmine or something of the sort behind an ear or tucked in their hair or between the teeth. The Prince's big fleshy brown body was bare to the waistline of his yellow sarong; but he wore, to mark his regality perhaps, a pair of European shoes. He was very handsome in a plump, young-middle-aged way, and bubbling with good humour, joking with the men and teasing the boys—who seemed to tease him back, but always using the idiom proper to his lofty station, while his remarks to them were made in their plebeian speech. Such was the etiquette at a Bali court. The Prince shook jovially with laughter at his own and the others' jokes; his fatty wobbling breasts quivered and his great stomach heaved like a bellows.

While gaily conversing, through the interpreter, with the Prince and his courtiers, I became aware of a warm, palpable presence against my shins and thighs, as if a great lazy dog were leaning against them; and, glancing down, found myself looking into a grinning coffee-brown face with a wide scarlet mouth behind bone-white teeth. He was squatting on the step against my feet, and his thin bare arms were folded comfortably over my knees—as if I'd been put there as a natural support for sprawling, lolling boys taking their ease. He seemed to me quite delightful, and perhaps about twelve years old—though a slight dark brown where his whiskers would be suggested he might be a year or two older. And who would blame my hand, of its own volition, it seemed—without waiting for instructions from me—for wandering down on to that glowing brown back, and feeling the warm undulations of its chocolate skin? The boy's grin became even more friendly, and he seemed to give a small affirmative toss of his head—"Go ahead," his expression appeared to say; and ahead I went.

Still brightly talking about such things as the rice-harvest in Bali and what people ate in England—"Yes, we do eat rice in England, but not every day"—I allowed my hand to do what it liked, and to descend to deeper levels of exploration : bending slightly as if to scratch my toe, I picked up the hem of his sarong and felt my fingers encircle first his ankle and then the warm yielding softness of his calf, and then the narrows of one thigh above the knee. . . .

I couldn't believe that the Prince—his chief interest at the moment being his foreign guest, he kept his good-humoured gold-flecked eyes fixed most of the time on me—hadn't noticed what I was up to; and the others, too, gathered on the steps couldn't have failed to observe my unusual movements. But nobody seemed to mind; I saw no sign that my behaviour was considered to be bad-mannered; so I didn't desist. . . . Most certainly the boy didn't mind : he shifted his position so that my hand could more easily glide up the yielding acres of his thigh and into the immense dark caverns of treasure that lay beyond. . . .

"Yes, yes, how fascinating—" I was saying to the Anuk Agung, as he recounted to me the various episodes of the thrilling Monkey Dance which was to be performed a few nights later—a show with a cast quite as big as that of any Broadway musical and with as much zip and zest; ". . . how fascinating—" I repeated; and, below, my knuckles came up against the silky folds of a lolling soft pouch of warm wrinkles; and then my fingers touched a velvety tuft like the down on a pigeon's breast—and then found themselves closing round a tense, upward straining rod that felt like a pillar of flame; as mighty and muscular, it seemed in my fevered mind, as the boy's entire body—a weapon of priapic proportions in the dark and secret fantasia beneath the sarong . . . "But fascinating, Prince, how I'm *longing* to see it"—but I wasn't thinking any longer of the Monkey Dance. . . .

After a pause, during which it may have appeared to the Prince that my attention had been wandering, he said : "You will be needing an attendant in your pavilion. I shall tell that young boy who's sitting there beside you to stay with you there tonight." What, I wondered, is the proper way to show one's gratitude for such exquisite hospitality?

*   *   *

It was a night of games rather than of passion—we were like children, I felt, told to run off and have a good romp. Romp we did; while the splendid torrential rhythms of the *gamelan* pounded below our windows; and then slept through the quick oblivious night and then awoke, both at the same instant, in the fresh bright twittering dawn, and smiled at each other, because we both felt so jolly.

Later that morning we joined the Prince for a walk to the sea; two or three of his retainers and half a dozen of the village boys came too. We went along the banked-up pathways between waterlogged paddy-fields, skirted tangles of mini-jungle and suger-palm and huge venerable banyans with multiple trunks like something out of space fiction; and heard the swish and chatter of the leaping monkeys high among the branches. Halfway, we rested in the shade of one of these; and the boys, running up like squirrels, scaled the fifty-foot bare trunks of neighbouring coconut palms to knock down some nuts so that we could all have a drink. The coconut glades, clumps of soaring stalks like a field full of ostriches, grew down to the very brink of the shore—there were fifty yards of golden sand between the green gables of the palm-forest and the big Pacific breakers.

From the water's brink one or two fishermen were casting with hand-nets into the surf—nets very like, I suppose, those familiar on the Sea of Galilee since's Peter's time, and exactly the same as I've seen on the banks of the Upper Niger near Timbuctoo. A few catamarans lay beached above the tide—very different frrom what are known today as "catamarans" in the yachting world : a single longboat with short mast and lugsail, and two outrigger spars fore and aft holding a hefty steadying beam or pole which acted as a second keel.

We'd all drop our sarongs, and dash down into the breaking rollers—led by the laughing plump Anuk Agung, whose fat flabby buttocks waggled as he ran and whose dangling genitalia were much too voluminous to keep within the cover of his veiling hand. The boys leapt and dived and surfaced like dolphins, and my little friend's slight brown form flashed over the water like a fish's fin.

Then we'd wander slowly back to Saba, cracking more nuts on the way and drinking the milk; and the Prince's household would send over to my pavilion palm leaf platters of rice and pork (the lean, hairy, untamed-looking pigs rootled round every village), which the boy and I ate together beside the shadowed pillars of our dwelling. And while we ate, the weirdly sweet notes of some aerial woodwind would come melodiously down to our ears : the Balinese are in the habit of rigging high among the branches a kind of flute-like contrivance which, when the breeze blows right, gives out soft dulcet sounds, a kind of airborne music. And then, once we'd eaten and digested, it was soon time for another romp. . . .

I stayed at Saba perhaps a week; we parted, that charming urchin and I, as lightheartedly as we had spent our time together. He was overjoyed at the new sarong I gave him.

*　　　*　　　*

On another visit to Bali, I gained a memory which has remained with me ever since, even more precious than that of my companion at Saba. I set off from Denpasar, the island's "business-centre," to visit an old friend, a Swiss artist who for a great many years had lived in a small village on the heights of the mountain : the great purple-crowned volcano which has since disastrously erupted. I have written elsewhere about what I met with during this ascent of the mountain, and might as well repeat now what I said then. The first paragraph reveals the Balinese belief in their key position in the universe :

"While the sun circled about the earth, the world, of

course, revolved round Bali; the Gunung Agung, the great central mountain, was the 'navel of the earth'; wherever one might be, one could always find the North by looking towards the mountain. . . .

"High on the mountain, Theo lived with his Balinese family: a delightful and talented Swiss painter and a kind of father-figure to his villagers: to him, possessed of useful medical knowledge, they brought their maladies as well as their domestic problems. His people were great brewers of *tuak*; and visiting him, one could be sure of a splendid roistering time and a performance of the dance special to his village: by which small dainty girls, crowned with flowers, exorcized the devils of anybody who chanced to be possessed of some. . . .

"On the way up to Theo's, there was a hamlet called Selatt, surrounded by terraced padi-fields. Here one stayed in a resthouse where, for a few *rupiya* one could get a dish of rice, a flagon of *tuak* and a small room; and where, after gently making known to the Mayor one's amorous preference, one's desires were mysteriously fulfilled. Nothing was said; nobody appeared during the evening's supping and drinking; but when one went to bed one would find, wistfully smiling from the gloaming of the room, a tender brown creature who took it for granted he was staying the night. There would be no question of payment: the Balinese weren't interested in money; but if one made a present of a new sarong there would be abounding and touching gratitude. That's how I came to know Ktut—alas, I have treacherously forgotten his name, for Ktut was merely his 'title,' meaning 'second son': one of the sweetest and most affectionate companions I've had, who stayed with me for all the rest of that blissful month and travelled with me all over the island. . . ."

So Ktut, of course, went with me up to Theo's; I remember how, walking up, we came high above the rice-fields to a mountain stream whose bed, though the river itself was little more than a trickle, was a broad ribbon of rock and boulder —washed clean of topsoil by centuries of recurring torrents. We picked our way upstream for quite a distance, jumping about the boulders: we wanted a pool at least deep enough to splash in, a freshener—after what had been a rather tumultuous night—before we arrived at Theo's. That night we slept happily together on a mat of plaited palm-leaf in a small room full of canvases and pots of paint; and next day went down to Denpasar.

I'd become good friends with the manager of the Denpasar Hotel, a shrewd, witty and understanding Dutchman: had I not know him well I don't suppose I'd have dared—though in those days I dared most things—to have Ktut staying in my hotel room for a week or so. But this nice man turned a blind eye on Ktut's presence, and the room-servants seemed to take him for granted. Ktut adored this strange sort of European luxury, and never tired of using the shower. But I didn't take him into the restaurant for meals: he went out to eat his own kind of food in the town. The sight of this golden-skinned fifteen-year-old clad only in a sarong taking his meals in the swagger restaurant would certainly have surprised most of the visitors there; but it was to save him embarrassment rather than myself that I didn't bring him in—he wouldn't have known how to go about this type of eating. But he often came in and joined me at my table while I was having a meal, and drank some orange juice or something—and it amused me to see my fellow customers stare!

We wandered together all over the island, staying in village inns and princely pavilions; and then I had to leave. I quote again:

"But then, like all one's loves made fleeting by the compulsions of time, bliss came to an end; I had to go back to work: I had to leave Ktut, pathetically forlorn, but enriched by several new sarongs and, I hope, some sweetness of memory. After sadly putting him on the bus for his home, I found that my aircraft was delayed and I had to stay for an extra bereaved day. In Powys Mathers' translation from the Arabian Nights: 'Were I to stay, I'd see the places where her absence is, And hear her silences: Let me away.' "

ISCHIA

I LIVED for a year or so on Ischia in 1952–53; but it was a few years earlier that I first set foot on the island : at the time when Burt Lancaster was making a film parodying romantic costumery, called *The Crimson Pirate*—I even sailed round in the pirate brigantine one day (the illusion only just survived the chugging of the engine) from the Port of Ischia to the little bay of Sant' Angelo, where some shooting was to be done.

At that time, Ischia was certainly the more attractive of the two islands that float like lightships across the Bay of Naples —three islands if one adds little Procida, flat but rather dull, nestling beneath Ischia's great tilted cone. While Ischia lacks the slightly operatic profile which encourages the simile "leviathan" to leap to the pen of writers about Capri, its silhouette, some may feel, is a more dramatic one, reaching up two thousand feet into the sky; and a more exciting one too : for, unlike Capri, which is a deadweight of limestone, Mount Epomeo is a dozing volcano—it violently erupted less than a century ago. Ischians say that Epomeo is connected with Vesuvius, some twenty miles away on the mainland, by a kind of submarine flue; and assert that when one mountain explodes the other will keep quiet. The people of Ischia therefore are always hoping that Vesuvius will blow up. . . . Another reason, of course, why Ischia, for people who like quiet, was then more agreeable than Capri was that the tourist trade hadn't properly discovered it; while the *piazzetta* of Capri was crammed with theatrical celebrities, visitors to Ischia arrived there almost by mistake.

Ischia's harbour is itself a circular volcanic crater which

time has filled up with the sea. Behind it the undistinguished town runs along a narrow hem of plain, hard against the dark-green background of the mountain slope.

I came, that first time, on a friend's yacht, and lived aboard for the week or so we were there. Half a dozen or more yachts were in the harbour but, although it was a brilliant September, there were few tourists.

Boys clustered round our gangplank, as boys always do in any port when foreign yachts arrive : hoping for cigarettes or the odd coin or chance employment on errands; or, not seldom, on the lookout for remunerative sexual adventure— this last, however, in Italy, more often in those days than now, when poverty and unemployment are less acute. A rather plain boy of about fourteen, with gentle manners and a ready sensuality, made friends and even sailed with us as extra "crew" as far as Palermo, returning home from there by the mail-steamer. His name was Attilio—though he would have been miscast in the role of Attila. And then, at the foot of a mountain track, I manoeuvred acquaintance with a comely bronze-haired boy of fifteen, who led me to a deserted cove of gigantic boulders, where crabs scuttled in the rocky pools and the short waves gurgled; but he came of a family of anarchists and was the opposite of devout. In my remaining days, he visited me aboard the boat, coming daily round the mountain from his village the other side of it. The village, he told me, was Forio, pronounced with the accent on the *i*; I hadn't heard the name before and, at the time, thought nothing more of it. . . .

Back on the island three or four years later, I remembered that an old friend, an American novelist, was living there; and when I learned that his house was at Forio, the name took me back in a flash to the caressing feel of soft bronze curls and a clear burnished skin like pale varnish—Rosario's curls and skin : he must be about nineteen now, I thought. And I took the bus over to Forio, on the north-west tip of the island, with expectations no more aspiring than lunch with my friend and a possible encounter with Rosario for old times' sake. I stayed in Forio for nearly a year.

There were two reasons : the natural beauty, and the amiability, of the place; and the lavishness of its boys— lavish, I mean, in numbers and lavish with their charms. It was at once obvious that in Forio there lived a tradition, one might almost call it Greek, of paedophilia—one was told, even of certain old baldheads, that they'd been, in their time, the boyfriend of this or that almost historical notability. It did seem, though, as I myself soon found out, that the boys were brought up, almost in the Hellenic fashion, to receive the attentions and benevolence of a grown man—or, at any rate, of a well-to-do foreign visitor.

At the base of the mountain, beneath the speckled bands above of olive and vine, the village rambled along the edge of an escarpment and ended in the little church of Our Lady of Succour, disarmingly crammed with childlike paintings of shipwreck and other marine disaster, the ex-voto offerings of fishermen. The church peered watchfully over the cliff into the waves swirling among a shambles of rock; and the village itself, propped up by a bastion of masonry falling a hundred feet or so to the beach, looked across at the massive seawall which encircled the fishing harbour, leaving open only a narrow entrance through which the daily steamer from Naples could creep to its anchorage. To tourists, one of the houses balanced above the beach was pointed out as the residence of two vicariously notorious widows, Rachele and Edda Mussolini, who after the collapse of fascism in Italy were obliged for a time to live on Ischia in a kind of political exile (ironically, Mussolini sent hundreds of his opponents to "obligatory sojourn," as the Italians put it, on nearly all the islands in Italian waters).

The inhabitants of Forio, except its shopkeepers and the people ministering to the Neapolitan holiday-making families who settled expansively down for a week or two every summer, besides essential craftsmen like stone-masons and cobblers, were engaged in catching or marketing fish—and the men who owned the fishing-boats and went to sea in them formed the aristocracy of the village. These men, with their wives and children, like all fishing people in Italy, seemed to a stranger an almost monkish confraternity—aloof, ungracious, curt, secretive, like an order of initiates (which they were), indifferent to anybody's interests but their own. They disdained "foreigners"; and thought very little of the wine-growers who lived and tended their vines up the mountain, men who had no understanding of the sea—and who, anyway, spoke a different dialect; and they were hardly on speaking terms with the people of Panza, a village three kilometres away who had their own dialect too. Fisherboys generally, bred to their fathers' code of stand-offishness, are hard to know; yet at Forio the paedophilist tradition seemed to flourish even in the enclosed fishing community, and while I was there I had four fisherboy friends—or rather three friends and an acquaintance (a slightly older brother of one of the friends).

In the summer the fine spread of sand below the village was taken over by the Neapolitans, whose enormous mothers and aunts sat like puffed-out broody hens in their drawers and chemises, exposing to the sun white mottled thighs like legs of outsize pork and unendingly eating peanuts; while their sons and nephews, with knowing naughty faces, like bronzes from Pompei, compared each others' sexual parts behind their elders' backs. Farther along to the west, the beach was the fishermen's: strangers strolling along it, if looked at at all, were scanned with an eyeful of displeasure by the family crews tinkering over their tipped-up boats or sewing at their nets: netmending, they held their needles, as big as bodkins, in their mouths like dressmaker's pins, when their hands were occupied, and kept the net taut with their bare big toes. It was here that the high-prowed boats were beached, coming in from fishing; propelled through the harbour entrance in long, convulsive strokes by two, three, four, even six oarsmen, standing to their sweeps and rowing in absolute unison of movement—grandfather and grandson working as equal parts of one perfectly precise machine. The women came down the hill when, watching from their rooftops, they sighted the family boat; and stood at the water's edge while the stern anchor was thrown out and—the boat standing in the shallows—the boxes of fish were handed ashore. Without losing a moment the boys of each crew, a box balanced on their heads or carried between two of them, set off for the village, crying their fish through the streets, the woodwind resonance of their refrain echoing among the houses like alleluias in a church. It was on this beach, too, that I first saw Gianni, and first heard him singing as he sat athwart the nets; one leg thrust forward and barefooted, his toes pegging the mesh where he wanted it, while he crocheted away at the tear with a sure handling of his cord and long wooden hook. Of Gianni's looks—handsome his face is, as I see it now, though without much sign of the human heart—I remember most clearly the faultless shaping of his head: why, one asks continually, can a centimetre more or less, this way or that, in life as in art, make the difference between perfection and the commonplace? Gianni's head was perfection: the classic boyish skull; the black wavy cropped hair; the ears and nape whose perfect fittingness caught one's breath, like the exactly felicitous musical phrase. He used to come bounding down the sandy, stony hill, singing at the top of his voice—the song swooping down behind his swift movement like a bird's; he'd go on singing the same familiar Neapolitan airs while he worked on the net: the air filled with his voice, whose pitch was more a trumpet's than a bugle's: no longer a treble, it wasn't yet an alto; and the harbour resounded with its notes as does a barrack-square with calls-to-the-cookhouse-door.

Near the sands where the nets lay spread, a breach like a gateway in the seawall gave on to the rocks and swirling gullies of the shore beyond. One morning, sunbathing here on the sand after a swim, I saw Gianni stand up from his net, thick working trousers rolled up to above the calf, and, still singing, walk over to the gap in the wall. He disappeared from view behind the mole, and the singing stopped: something was interesting him enough to quell even his voice. I could guess what he might be doing: the temptation to make sure was too great; I followed him round to the rocks behind the breakwater. It was a bright day with the sky of golden blue and a glistening cobalt sea; a fair north breeze was whipping the surf into clouds of white spray over the brown-black rocks. I found him standing on a broad black rock: a flesh-white silhouette against a curtain of blue sea, garlanded with spray; his trousers were coiled round his ankles and his shirt was pulled up to his neck: and irresistibly attracting the eye like a magnet, his "fish" was standing dominantly up on its tail, as if everything else within sight were subordinate to this impudent adolescent feature. (*Pesce*—fish—is the popular Neapolitan word for penis—such an exactly descriptive appellation that one's surprised its use isn't more widespread. But I've met it only in and around Naples: most districts of

Italy have their own local term, besides the general slang word *cazzo*: in Apulia, for example, the word is *pizza*—which in Naples is a speciality of the kitchen.) It was a fine fish, large as a good-sized mackerel; and rose from a groin of pearl-pale flesh, between unfurling tufts of dark down. Gianni was plainly proud of his fish: he was looking down at it with affection, while with his right hand he pulled its resistant length downwards as far as it would go, and let it flick back again like a catapult against his belly. . . .

Suddenly he knew he was being silently watched, and looked nervously over his shoulder; but when he saw I was a foreigner he visibly relaxed—foreigners, all the boys knew, did this sort of thing themselves! So, having seen who it was, he went on with his game, glancing over now and again to give me a reassuringly jolly grin. And then I was following him as best I could over the rocks along the length of the seawall, he scampering over them like a goat while with both hands he held his trousers round his waist. He'd known every crevice of this shore from childhood: every rock and every boulder, every ledge and foothold: he was far ahead when, towards the end of the breakwater where the light-house marked the harbour entrance, he halted, waiting for me—poised and graceful even when holding up his trousers. When I caught up with him, he made for a gap between two rocks which seemed little different from any other, but which he picked out with the certainty of a dog seeking out a buried bone; and between these rocks he disappeared. Down the gap I followed. We were in a kind of grotto, invisible from above but below at once roomy and compact, as if scooped out by some giant bulldozer from the sea and roofed over with great boulders fitted one against the other like a piece of Cyclopean masonry. The waves growled and gulped beyond the seaward wall of the chamber; the flooring was of level rock standing in a few inches of crab-rippled water, and there was a snugly shaped boulder which might have been specially hewn to receive the forms of two persons who didn't mind being cramped. . . . Reclining upon it, with his cropped curly head and slightly satanic charm, his naked body pearly pale against the damp gloom of the rocks, in a silence eerie but for the drip and squelch of water, Gianni put me in mind of some urchin-attendant upon Neptune—a boy-nereid, if there were such a creature, with seaweed twined in his hair and a fish between his legs. . . . I've said already that the expression of Gianni's features, handsome and swarthy, seemed heartless; and his heart, I soon discovered, worked without emotion : his flesh was full of bounding blood and clamorous sensuality, but the heart that made it all go was like a plastic one. The instant our moments of concord were over he changed from being the limp, clinging, swim-ming-eyed swooner he'd just been and became the man of business : Double it ! he said curtly when I proffered a fairly generous gift : double it, was his motto : two cigarettes instead of one, a thousand lire instead of five-hundred. . . . I often saw Gianni after that, on the beach or in the village : he was an amusing person, and I got a great deal of pleasure out of looking at him. Nearly every day the harbour would fill with his singing, and I would hear him run down the hill to work on the nets. As the months went by and he grew older I noticed with an absurd regret that the pure trumpet clarity of his voice was beginning to roughen. I never went again to Wankers' Cave. , . .

*　　*　　*

The writer through whom I first came to Forio was one of a small group of Americans, British and Germans, mostly engaged professionally or playfully in one or other of the arts, who lived in or near the town; and through them the place had become known among foreign "intellectual" coteries and its fame spread into queer ones. But at that time the great invasion by cackling cohorts of international queer-dom hadn't yet begun; although beach and piazza were already dottied and dotty enough with gay little swimming trunks of leopard-skin or pale blue satin; and Maria's bar shrilled with the cosmopolitan queens' speech.

These visitors, for the most part, were blond and pink-skinned; they'd come from the then puritanical North, either coupled off in quest of a cosy honeymoon in the sun or else bursting to let their hair down in the most egregiously un-Nordic behaviour. Those not already paired off, came seek-ing whom they could devour among the Forian youth. The summer thus brought to Forio two entirely separate "foreign" intrusions, between which there was no contact (except per-

129

haps for casual sex): the sprawling yowling Neapolitan holiday-making families, and the shrieking, coquetting Euro-
American queers: both made a lot of noise, each of their
own kind. Between them, they filled up the three or four
pensioni Forio possessed and the sprinkling of houses and
apartments kept empty by their owners for the "season." I
came before the main body of the seasonal arrivals, and
within a week or two I'd found, with the help of two boys
and of Maria herself (she was said to accomplish any sort
of procuration asked for by a good customer), a charming
little Arab-style house above the piazza, for a very moderate
rent: "Arab" I call it, because it was built on the Saracen
model still followed on the island though ten centuries and
more had passed since it was introduced by the African invaders. It was engagingly pretty, with vaulted stone Arab
ceilings washed, like the the walls below it, in the soft cerulean
known locally as "Forian blue"; but it wasn't really designed
or fitted out for comfort: the lower floor was like a huge
derelict dungeon, in a corner of which was the complicated
charcoal cooking-stove; on the first floor were to be found,
if one looked, a number of dusty, crumbling rooms, peopled
by spiders and blackbeetles, into which nobody would dream
of going—and one large sparsely furnished room opening on
to a pleasant balcony: a balcony which proved a great
convenience when Franco became my squire and house-
keeper. Through a kind of hatchway from the first-floor landing, the roof could be reached: a perfect setting for photo-
graphing boys—an exciting and rather dangerous-looking
labyrinth of gutters and parapets and concavities: all scrambling around the base of a tiny dome like a miniature St.
Peter's and all seeming to peer perilously down to the street
below.

Before I found this house, a number of boys had introduced
themselves to me, because I was a foreign visitor and therefore must be expected to want to meet boys; some, of course,
had been agreeable yet ephemeral; there'd been three more
fisherboys besides Gianni, and two or three among the band
of schoolboys who daily took the boat across to Procida,
where there was a nautical school. But my interest in none of
them went beyond curiosity: that satisfied, I didn't want to
see them again. After all, it was they who came knocking at

my door : not the other way about. But one of them, who anyhow was never more than a sort of camp-follower of the others (he was much too small to arouse even my sexual inquisitiveness), seemed to be always about—he came to my door, asking for errands to be run, shopping to be done and so on; and I found myself becoming rather unwillingly fond of him, as one can get fond of a stray dog that wags its tail. His name, very inappropriately, was Santino; he was cheeky, wicked, monkey-faced, ready for every sort of mischief, and looked no older than eleven. When I asked him why he didn't go to school and what his father had to say about his hanging around a foreigner, he replied : "Oh, my father likes me to come to see you. He says : 'What have you come home for? Go and do anything that foreigner wants—and then you can bring some money home.' " It was Santino's energy and terrier-like perseverance that discovered my new house and secured Maria's help. And it was Santino who brought Franco to me—without Santino's skilful agency I might have got no nearer to Franco than making eyes at him.

Franco, for some time, had been a tantalizing decoration in the background of the boys I knew : a boy whose very stand-offishness made him the more desirable; he was given to blushing, and sheepish grins, and, I was told, stubbornly refused to be mixed up with foreigners. He was of fishing descent; but there was no longer a family boat, and his father now did odd jobs ashore. So did Franco, in principle; he preferred, however, comfortable repose to physical exertion and (as I found later) had an insatiable appetite for the sensual pleasures, if he could enjoy them without making too much effort himself : his theory, I think, was the excellent one that there are few things in life more worthwhile doing than nothing. Now and then I would see him, probably together with Santino, pushing a handcart up from the jetty where packing-cases, barrels and sacks and been unloaded from the Naples boat. But the earnings from one of these excursions gave him a day or two of doing nothing—he ate at home and only needed to buy cigarettes—until it was time for another trip with the handcart. Franco was tall and yet moved as gently as a cat; he had big, strong shoulders but those hips, you felt, you could hold in your hands; fair Nordic hair tumbled over a clear English face. He was obviously a Norman : one of the heirs, such as one often sees in southern Italy, of those marauding barons who a thousand years ago turned from murder and brigandage to the most splendid kingship. It was doubtless from some of the later, more effete strains of Norman blood that Franco drew his love of indolence and lazy ease, and, if he could have achieved it, or knew about such things, of sybaritic luxury. But when he found I was looking at him, he blushed and dropped his eyelids like a bashful girl; or even stood up and moved aloofly away—he knew what I was after but wasn't playing. . . .

I've said that Franco's face was "English"; yet that wasn't what distinguished it—it was those infinitesimal fragments of millimetres which, filling the curve of the jaw here, fining down a nostril there, can transform mediocrity into the superlative. One cannot define the human face or analyse human beauty; one simply knows instinctively when those millimetre touches of transcendent style create a face that haunts and compels.

But Franco's response when I made my tentative advances, was to look bashful, or turn his eyes away in dismissal, or get up and crushingly walk off. Even when I offered him a cigarette, he pretended he didn't want to smoke—a sacrifice almost unthinkable to any Italian boy. He met me every time with a snub—and, of course, putting myself in his shoes, I entirely understood his attitude. And then Santino arranged it : Santino, with his mischievious, monkey-nosed charm. Probably it happened on the spur of the moment, which is the way boys do things, rather than by design; but however it was, they appeared together one morning at my house : where, for ten minutes, Franco sat blushing and tongue-tied, smirking and cracking his knuckles. Then I sent them both out to buy *pasta* and beefsteak and watermelon; and when they came back set them to cooking us all a meal. Next day they came again; and a habit was formed—without anybody's mentioning anything, they were coming daily, as a matter of course, to do the shopping and to eat. Franco wouldn't allow Santino out of his sight—he seemed still appalled by the idea of being left alone with me; but he enjoyed, in an indolent and perhaps feminine way, doing the cookery and giving Santino the jobs that needed exertion—and he enjoyed going shopping, the feel of money in his hand and the power of spending it. Franco always brought back the exact change, and was obviously charging the proper prices—while Santino, whenever he'd done some marketing, had always added a bit on for himself : reciting his list of inflated prices with an engaging smile of innocent deceit.

I used to watch Franco's face while he was happily busy in the kitchen, unconcerned and unselfconscious—fanning the charcoal into a glow beneath the steak being grilled, or breaking up the *pasta* to go with the beans. His eyes had the grey-blue tincture of the sea off the Normandy coast, the eyebrows so fair as to be almost invisible; and, what's so common among boys of the North but rare in the South, he seemed to be without lashes. Somehow this enhanced his look of defencelessness : there's many a faint-hearted boy who shelters behind a pair of lush eyelashes. Franco's vulnerability seemed to me more a childish *need* : some *lack* was delineated in the softness of the line of his jaw and cheek and in the silky gold at the back of his neck—it was the helplessness of an egg without a shell. He needed, I thought, mothering. Surely, too, this indolence, this weary languor—what most people would call downright laziness—must really be less a fault of character than of metabolism : a sloth that yelled for protein. So I made up my mind to give him some mothering : he should have all the beefsteak he could eat, even if he refused to have affection too. . . .

And then one afternoon, while I was writing beside the big window that opened on to my balcony, my mind was suddenly alert to a sort of non-sound : I looked up, and there was Franco standing on the balcony with a small disarming smile. He'd swarmed up from the street below with the sound-lessness of a squirrel. I was so taken aback that, instead of bursting into excited welcome, I could only say : "Why didn't you knock at the door?" He answered, with a weary shrug : "It's less trouble this way—less of a bore than banging away at the knocker and waiting." Then he walked into the room and eyed the bed and the only other chair. "I think I'll lie on your bed, if I may," he announced. "I'm tired—I want to stretch out; and it's so hot and dusty out of doors. But I think I'll take a shower first—" and he began to strip his clothes off, throwing them on to the floor beside the bed. Then, quite naked, he sauntered off to the staircase and down to the groundfloor lobby where I'd made the boys fix up a makeshift shower . . . . I could only gape at the gleaming white body, and with its patina of golden down, and at the sweet rueful face; and gape at the astonishing, the impossible fact that he'd come and the comical manner of his coming, and gape at this new and baffling manifestation of the incomprehensibility of boys generally and of Franco in particular. . . .

After that, he showed up each afternoon, offering no explanation and I asking for none: he might have been coming to my house all his life, for all the sign he made. I'd be sitting working beside the window or on the balcony when I'd hear his strident errand-boy whistling far down the long street from the piazza—a whistling that became a habit every day, something to watch out for, a landmark in time, like the ringing of the angelus: it was nearly always half past two when I heard the whistle—he had an almost animal instinct for the hour and then my ears would follow his whistle up the long street and I'd see him come into view over the hillcrest below the house: a loose, easy-going figure, lithe yet lazy, dressed in torn white shirt and stained blue cotton trousers—one sandal, probably, broken and hanging on by a toe. Softly as a lizard he'd run up the wall, using handholds I couldn't see, and swing himself over the balcony with languorous ability. (I protested that he was setting a bad example: that thieves would climb into the house and steal my typewriter. He replied that nobody on Ischia could climb as he could and no other boy would dare to try to reach my balcony.) I found myself waiting and watching for him—and of relishing, already in the early morning, the coming pleasure of watching for him in the afternoon. The sound of his whistling became a thing of beauty in itself: I haven't ceased to hear it yet.

He lay on the bed as if lying down were a luxurious act of subsidence, his body, with all his bones and muscles united solely for this pleasure, seemed to be trying to sink ever more deeply into the sensuous laxity of the bed. He was at his happiest when surrendering himself utterly to both physical sensation and physical comfort, ecstatically yielding to the delights of the two together to the exclusion of all other consciousness: he delighted above all in the sensation of touch, of *feeling*, of being touched; motionless, except for little reflex movements of pleasure, he would want me to stroke and caress the whole surface of his body, from the top of his head to the tip of his toes—he would moan with pleasure, and sigh, and make little incredulous gestures with a hand, as if protesting that such heights of sensual joy couldn't exist. . . . And now and then he'd murmur small phrases of endearment, like a child dreaming: *ti voglio bene, ti voglio bene.* . . . Franco told me, after some weeks of this, that for years he had daily masturbated at least twice, often three times; but that since these afternoon entries by way of the balcony, he'd been content with once—and that without his having to exert himself at all. Franco didn't easily find words in which to express just what was in his mind; but I made out that he found an emotional satisfaction in the partnership of our joint eroticisms—he'd always felt, he said, as if there were something missing from the pleasure of his solitary "saw" (*far' la sega*—the Neapolitan colloquialism for masturbation).

This went on for nearly a year. Every day I listened for his whistle; every day he swung himself silently over the balcony. . . . I never understood Franco, but I became enormously fond of him : as one is fond of a sweet, loyal creature that depends upon one. I never discovered what caused that abrupt and total reversal of his attitude towards me—what turned contemptuous hostility to a touching and even devoted submission.

But the end had to come : work took me away from Ischia, and I have never seen Forio again. When I think of the place, I get a flood of memories; but clearer than all is the sound of Franco's whistling coming up from the piazza.

SAIGON AND HANOI

When I read about Saigon in the newspapers, I think of the Saigon I knew just twenty years ago; and I see a tricycle —or rather dozens or hundreds of tricycles, and one in particular; and when I read the name Hanoi, I see a dainty, serpentine, willow-pattern sort of little lake, like a Chinese painting of a lake, with a diminutive pagoda at the tip of a minute promontory.

The tricycles in Saigon were in fact rickshaws—at least an improvement, from the point of view of human suffering, on the old kind drawn by men padding along on foot between shafts (there were still some of these, at that time, to be hired in Malayan or Indonesian towns); the passenger sat on a sort of invalid-chair slung between the two front wheels so that, unless he twisted his head round from front to back, he could have no idea what the steersman behind him was up to; and being whirled nose first, so to speak, among the traffic his sole sensation and preoccupation was a terrifying helplessness—the sort of helplessness of a man who loses his voice in the moment of needing to cry "Help!" These three-wheeled juggernauts were propelled mainly, it seemed, by pubescent boys and old men with legs all shin and gristle; and were owned by a handful of capitalists who paid these wretches a meagre living for doing the work of mules or motors. Just at that time a few tricycles were indeed running with motors— as novel a sight to the Saigonese as Bleriot's airplane was to the British and French in 1910: the rickshaw was becoming mechanized, an innovation which, bringing incalculable benefit to the rickshawmen, made for the passenger even the briefest of journeys a madman's nightmare. The one particular tricycle was ridden by a lanky Annamite waif in his early adolescence : I dare say he'd reached fourteen. How odd one's memory is—or rather, how strange that some impressions made on it, seemingly so light and casual at the time, should turn out to be imperishable. . . .

My visits to French Indo-China (the name Vietnam had just come in, I think, for the southern half of the country, with a nominal independence under the "emperor" Bao Dai) were far too filled up with work for me to go around looking for sexual adventure or emotional intimacy; but even the busiest of men can't help things happening. I resisted the temptations of the shoeshine boys who flocked like sparrows in the *place du théâtre* : an ample airy square linking the chief hotel—the Continental, was it called?— with the main street and the waterfront. The theatre stood like a church : a lofty piece of colonial-Parisian architecture, empty and neglected and ignored, except by the shoeshine boys who slept in its porches and played on the plinth of steps that magniloquently encircled it. I wonder if this sad edifice has opened its doors at all in the last twenty years of perpetual war? I wonder when it will next—if, indeed, it's still standing? War of a sort was being fought then : a war of bombs in the towns and guerrilla hide-and-seek in the swamps and paddy-fields : the war of Vietnam nationalists against the French, with, up in Tonkin, Ho Chi Minh running it; in Saigon explosions were fairly common and hotels and restaurants had wired their windows against lobbed-in bombs. But it was a very small war compared with what has come to the country since. . . . Then, the theatre stood forlornly, and yet with the air of an old prima donna who had her memories of applause; and under its walls the shoeshine boys sheltered. The square was deployed beneath its facade; and somewhere within the complexity of streets behind it, I remember, there was incongruously the "rue Roodyarr' Keeplang"—I used to wonder why Rudyard Kipling, the bard of British imperialism, should be commemorated on a street-sign in a French colonial town —or did the French honour him as the pure spirit of colonialism?

I suppose I could have picked any one of the shoeshine boys; there was one attractive lad who daily fought the others off to work on my shoes—on the first day I'd given him much more than the usual fee because he had a pretty face and a sweet smile; he was reproachfully disappointed whenever I came to the square wearing sandals. . . . They were delightful boys, these elfin guttersnipes : engaging and good-natured and full of fun; but if one looked a little behind the fun, one could see the tragic marks of homelessness and hunger on their near-childish faces, and the bitter pathos of boyhood without love. All of them, I don't doubt, were proficient in the tricks of extortion and adept in every category of sin : yet I was certain, too, that affection and kindness, plus vitamins and protein, could have salvaged any one of them. But I hadn't got time : I was ham-strung by the compulsions and conventions of making a living : I didn't dare run the risk of finding myself made responsible by love. . . . Where are they now, those sparrows of the theatre square?

When, in the daytime, I had a spare hour which I could pleasantly waste, I would walk down to the waterfront, to a point in the bend of the Saigon River where the British legation stood. Further down the river, to the right, lay the docks where berthed, after their thirty-mile run upstream from the coast, the ocean steamers that still came to Indo-China, running the gauntlet of the guerrilla bullets that often sprayed them from the river-banks : ships of the Messageries Maritimes and the Paquet line, chiefly carrying reinforcements for the Foreign Legion and military material. A little way to one's left stood the wooden pier which, jutting out into the river like something at Brighton, supported an excellent restaurant that was a favourite of the French and other foreigners and of the Saigonese bourgeoisie. At the point where I chose to stand, leaning over above a narrow strip of muddy shore and gazing at the dark sluggard of a river which swirled slowly by, there were some rafts moored, connected with the shore by a rickety length of duckboarding, and used, so far as one could see, by nobody besides the innumerable boys who disported themselves there. The prospect beyond was beautiful, in the kitchen-sink manner; the sluggish, yellow river and general waterfront squalor; the decay and sadness of the war-neglected buildings and the dreary empty warehouses; the smoky silhouettes of the clustered ships, seen through a Turneresque mist of humid heat. Here, as I stood watching at the water's edge, I used to wonder what the

British Minister, should he be peering out of his office window in a moment of unofficial repose, might think I could be up to, standing there for so long in the torrid afternoon. He was a nice fellow himself, and probably didn't give it a thought; but it tickled me to find this ribald scene set immediately below the Legation windows: British embassies, thought of as a whole and not broken down into their constituent members (who are usually charming people), are known to be the stuffiest places going, with the possible exception of American embassies.

The scene was the old and simple one which, until a century or so ago, had always occurred with the conjunction of warmth, water and boyhood: a hundred-odd boys, aged everything between seven and seventeen, bathing and romping naked and utterly unashamed and uninhibitedly performing, in full view of any of the public who happened to be about, every kind of bodily function you can think of. Now and then a chase, or follow-the-leader, or merely a boisterous stampede started by an explosion of spirits, would take a few dozen of them, bollock-naked, racing along the boulevard and through the side streets or around the extraterritorial walls of the British legation. Sometimes the frenchified Saigonese police would half-heartedly give chase, or occasionally even arrest one or two of them; but generally nobody bothered about them—to any French who saw them, they were *indigènes,* "natives"; to the natives—well, what did it matter? A century or more ago, scenes something like this, though perhaps on a less extravagent scale, occurred when the climate was right wherever there was water—in the river, by the dockside, among the seashore rocks; and even in the "civilized" view of Western society male nudity, so long as no females were about, was considered a normal and even "healthy" custom (look at the swimming-bath practice in most English public schools). But during the last century the bathing-pants complex has spread all over Europe and a large part of the Orient—actively encouraged, of course, by the drapers and haberdashers and manufacturers of "swimwear"; with the result that we've been made prurient by our acquired prudery, and the sight of nakedness elicits giggles, concupiscence, or police prosecution.

This, then, was my pastime, when I could snatch a spare

hour for dallying by the riverside and watching the charming scene which the British legation could observe from its windows every hour of its working day. But even the busiest of people can't help things happening. . . .

It was a tricycle rickshaw that caused the happening to me. I'd found a lodging just north of the cathedral—wherever I newly arrive, I try as quickly as possible to dodge out of the dictatorship of a hotel, preferring the humblest liberty to the most expensive discipline. This was a single little room at the top of a turret stair—an unlikely place to find in a French colonial town; it was almost empty of furniture and had no "conveniences" beyond the two important ones that it had its own shower and possessed what the French gracefully call *entrée libre* and the Germans more bluntly describe as *sturm-frei*—"storm-free" : free, that is, from officious regard for one's coming and going.

Here I brought my tricycle boy. I'd found him waiting on a rickshaw-stand at the far end of the luxuriant jungle-green gardens which confined the governor-general's *palais*—today, I believe, the President's. I chose him because he was the youngest : not influenced by any ulterior hope but simply because, given my natural fondness for the male young, I naturally wanted to help feed him that day rather than one of his elderly colleagues on the rank. So I hired him; he pedalled me to my lodging; and I paid him—overpaid him, a bit—and thought no more about him, or so I believed. Yet that night I did think about him, as one does think about boys one's seen (or girls, I suppose, when they're appropriate) : I found myself thinking about the curve of his rounded jaw, the brown softness of his look, the specially slender grace of his narrow loins. . . . And next day, the very next day (as if fate were working on the fact that my time in Saigon was running short), in quite a different part of the town, I looked round for a rickshaw, and there this boy was, at that moment cruising slowly by, leisurely pedalling, his slim buttocks alternately heeling over the saddle as his weight shifted from pedal to pedal. The magic of his smile of recognition left me without the power of choice.

Wooing, like any art, requires its appropriate instruments, its paints and brushes, paper and ink; for the dance, scope for the limbs and eyes. This last—latitude for meaning looks, for caressing movements of the hand—is, too, what wooing needs: it's difficult to make any sort of emotional approach when one has one's back to the beloved unable to gaze or converse; and when, for the moment, one's safety hangs upon the vigilance and skill of the beloved pedalling furiously behind one's back. As, that day, he propelled me through the streets of Saigon towards my attic lodging, while I sat clutching the sides of my hurtling chair and wondering how I could declare my passion, when we got there, in the minute or two of fumbling for the fare, my mind wandered for a moment, I remember, to Karachi, in Pakistan, where approach is easier to one's charioteer. There, an evening's promenade through the curry-scented dusk in one of those one-horsed victorias can be given an extra pinch of spice by standing up on the floor of the carriage and placing one's arms round the waist of the boy-cabman on the box—he is unlikely to show surprise. . . .

Yet these things arrange themselves. I can't now remember just how it came about: but there he was at the top of the turret stair, and there was the tricycle at the bottom, parked in the small courtyard. His French went little further than the addresses his passengers wanted to be taken to; and I wasn't able to find out much about him. I discovered that his real home, if he ever had one, was in Annam, that middle country between Tonkin and Cochinchina where the women are so exquisitely chic in white satin trousers beneath slit skirts, but I never learned how he came to be alone in Saigon. But there occur situations in which communication is possible without such aids as language. . . . To me, after he'd found out I was British, he would say: "Okay, you bastard"—apparently he thought this was the English way of saying *monsieur*. "Okay, you bastard," he would exclaim gaily when I named the place I wanted to go to; "okay, you bastard," if I indicated it would be nice to go to bed. I felt a slight jealousy when I allowed myself to conjecture that some American must have known him well enough to teach him "okay, you bastard". . . .

He was skin and bone, and pitifully narrow-framed for his height. Beneath the native glow of his pallor there was that faintly lemon opalescence, like gaslight seen through frosted glass, which comes with persistent underfeeding to the young of the Far East. He was as tall as a man, with a boy's body—he can't have been more than fourteen or fifteen; and seemed built of bone and sinew: thigh muscles swollen like the leg of a skinned lamb's carcass, and the flat of his stomach hard as a boat's deck. And yet he had a surprising grace and daintiness: the easy languor of a vine run riot; and under the shower he was a delight to look at—his body was almost without a hair. He had the Far Eastern love of cleanliness, and began every visit by tearing off singlet, shorts and sandals—all he ever wore—and wallowing under the shower. The beauty of his face was saved, so fleshless was it, from being the beauty of a skull by the natural fullness of both his boyhood and his race, and by the liveliness of his smile. The pathos of this body, this pinched, gay face, meant that half of my infatuation was pity—I suppose that all love, to a degree, contains pity: sexual love, to purify it of sheer carnality, requires compassion; and inert compassion is made dynamic by love. The vigour of one's compassion can reduce the other's unhappiness so long as there's no separation but when the parting comes, only money can help. I had to leave and, alas, when the time came and travel tickets and so on had been paid for, there was little cash left—but what there was, helped.

I never properly mastered his name; I could never properly explain why my compassion had to be cruelly withdrawn. I don't suppose he even wondered: for him, life was a row of unrelated parentheses, without a story.

That tricycle down in the courtyard, parked there day after day, must have puzzled a lot of people: a stray tricycle, "unattended," as the police say.

*   *   *

In Hanoi, one had the feeling of being in a different country; and so Tonkin does seem—as different from South Vietnam as Burma is from Siam; one may perhaps unify the two politically, as they were then supposed to be under French rule, but ethnologically they'll never become one. The people of Hanoi, up north towards the China border, were, as I remember them, rather Chinese than "southeast Asian": bigger-boned, perhaps, their eyes set deeper in their heads, and clothes more in the Chinese mode.

The picture I get at this distance of time from the syllables "Hanoi" is of a lake: a small, curling, carefully drawn lake with a stone bridge at one end, green parkland around it, and pleasantly eccentric trees bending from its banks over the water: a willow-pattern style of lake—and I suspect that the trees were willows. For the sake, perhaps, of artistic symmetry, the lake at its other end was furnished with an elegant and diminutive pagoda, built on the tip of a short causeway running out from the shore. Here, inside this temple, I met the small and vivacious Tonkinese who became my companion during the couple of weeks of my stay. I'd wandered aimlessly along the causeway, and finding the portals of the pagoda open, had ventured in, supposing the place to be empty.

Inside this temple, it was, beside a gleaming brass image—Buddha, perhaps or Confucius or Lao-tsze: I'm shamefully vague about these systems of worship; inside the temple, it was, that I kissed this unknown acolyte—who, from his eagerness, seemed to have been waiting some thirteen years or so for this moment. Afterwards, thinking about this impious embrace, I recalled a letter written by Oscar Wilde from, I think, Naples, in which he tells Robert Ross with some relish how, visiting a church, he kissed a seminarist behind the High Altar. I've often thought it probable that Wilde, with an eye to posterity and a roguish desire to *épater les bourgeois,* invented this situation—artistically, it would have appealed to him as a decorative jibe at those who ruined him. But I didn't invent this embrace: it was given impetuously amid the odour of smouldering incense and the crimson shadows of a dim, hushed chamber, full of vague hangings and the glint of metal vessels, and faintly lit by great swaying oil lamps—it was given by a strange small bare-footed boy, shaven-headed and wearing loose and not very clean Chinese-style trousers and jacket: he was eager to go beyond a mere kiss, but I didn't know what the penalties for flagrant sacrilege might be—at any moment some bonze or sacristan might silently glide in. . . .

I took him to my hotel, the most important of the European sort in the town, full of French officers, American diplomats, newspapermen of various countries, and prosperous Vietnamese conspirators—and through the crowded foyer to my room. Nobody seemed surprised, or asked him what his business was. . . .

TIMBUCTOO

ONCE, IN the zoo at Karachi, then the chief city of Pakistan, I stood for an hour with about a thousand other people watching the copulative exertions of a very old lion. The lioness was willing enough; and the male, though senility appeared to have made him a bit wobbly on his legs, was so eager for the enjoyment he hoped for even if he was too old to have it, that he had a go five times in that hour: after ramming away for a while and apparently bringing it to a glorious and phrenetic end, he would rest briefly in a corner, licking his chops; and then, tottering over the floor of the cage, he would mount his mate again. This happened five times in sixty-odd minutes.

This was interesting enough: it was the first time I had ever watched a love-making lion; but more interesting still I found the great crowd of spectators. It was one of those circular cages, so that nearly everybody massing round the safety-rail, and watching with fascinated, bemused eyes, had a splendid view. It was an audience of males—this is a Muslim country where women didn't at that time go much to the zoo anyway—about half of them grown-up, and half boys of all ages. There was no sniggering among the boys, as there would have been, say, in England, where a natural act—at least until very recently—wasn't decent; instead, there was a kind of solemnity, even reverence, as if they were participating in a sacramental rite. And, of course, they were: this was the fertility rite *par excellence* : this was not only Priapus *doing,* but Priapus *seen* to be doing. This was the eternal and mysterious and ever-awe-inspiring process of regeneration, the symbol of the unending cycle of the earth's renewal, being visibly and physically enacted publicly and, as it were, ceremonially; that, I believe, is what this silent, solemn, almost worshipful congregation were subconsciously feeling. This spectacle seen in the company of a thousand of one's fellows acquired a mystical significance that had nothing to do with having one's wife in bed or with going to the brothel. This was a *rite* : acts witnessed or performed in association with numbers of others always assume a meaning greater than themselves : eating by oneself is merely the consumption of food : a dinner-party is a ceremony : the Mass is a sacrament—and so on. And so it was with the public copulation of the king of beasts : it was the fertility rite performed with living blood and sperm—not merely a sacerdotal representation of it.

In northern Europe, and doubtless in America, because of a long history of puritan infection, like haemophilia in royal families, a conspicuous portion of the public's interest in animal lecheries is prurience : adults avert their eyes from a pair of shagging dogs in the street with a primness secreting a longing to look; while the youngsters, depending on the degree of surveillance, either titter and leer or furtively gloat. Further to the South in Europe, where the mating of animals isn't considered improper, the lubricious element becomes less obtrusive in the onlooker's eye and the "mystical," if one may use the word, takes over : there's a fascinated, and more objective, interest in the cryptic sexual processes without the dirty emotion of the puritans. About ten years ago in the zoo in Rome, at the further end of the Borghese gardens (so many years after Karachi, that poor old lion must have long been dead), a pair of black bears happened, when I passed their cage, to be focusing all their faculties of mind and sense on the act of coition : they had no nose free for buns or bananas. Nobody in the world, I suppose, is more sexually inflammable than the young Roman; yet the half-dozen Italian boys grouped round the cage were watching the operation with a dispassionate, speculative—almost academic— concentration, as if in it somehow they might find the key to an eternal mystery. A boy of sixteen, however, who was standing by himself and had hair of a fairness which I took to be Scandinavian or north German, was so visibly aroused and agitated that he couldn't keep his right hand still in his pocket.

On the island of Cyprus, off the shore of Turkey and the Lebanon, I received a few years ago yet another object lesson in the principles of sexual upbringing—and within the same context of animal conjugation. I got it while motor-scooting along that narrow pole-like peninsula, known as the "pan-handle," which runs out for several miles at a tangent from the north-east corner of the island. It's a wild sliver of country, low hills and slinky valleys, almost uninhabited and given up to tobacco-growing and the pasturing of great herds of goats.

The day I'm recalling must have fallen at the very peak of the goat-rutting season. I'd been driving slowly and quietly; cresting a hill I found myself looking into a long green valley, with no soul in sight except for three swarthy goatherds in early adolescence—I guessed they were all around thirteen and fourteen. They were sprawling in the shade of a carob tree, languidly playing some gambling game with pebbles; they were giving none of their attention to the goats, which swarmed in a vast kaleidoscopic flock all over the valley, mingling and moving and perambulating (at first glance) like the kinetic concourse in St. Mark's Square in Venice. But at second glance, it clearly wasn't like that at all. There appeared to be almost as many billy-goats as nannies; and all the nannies seemed to be in heat. All over the valley the males were screwing or fighting each other for the next nearest screw; or, having terminated one, were making for another with extended pintle protruding red and rigid like a cere-monial wax candle. There was one huge lout of a he-goat, as big as a pony; with tall spiralling horns, matted long hair like a yak's, and testicles so enormous and pendulous that the scrotum like an elongated udder brushed while swinging against the ground—a Great God Pan of a goat with whom none of the mere satyrs and sileni of the herd dared compete. They snatched a grind where Pan was not, or where he'd just been. I never thought I should live to see such an orgiastic glut of mass lechery, so grandiose a saturnalia of non-stop randiness. One quails before a guess at how much caprine sperm was shed that day. And all the time the three vigorous young goatherds lay quietly in the sun, shooting craps with pebbles and not giving so much as a glance at their riotously fornicating flock. A group of British boys of the same age, exposed to this thrillingly pornographic spectacle, would have been roused to such a pitch of erotic fret that they'd have embarked on a daylong orgy of mass masturbation.

But the Cypriot boys, besides regarding the mating of goats as a part, similar to the formation of the olive's fruit, of the seasonal round, had grown up with the spectacle—*they were used to it*. I have an idea that for those educational theorists who hold that prudery and puritanical blinkers are the surest safeguard against the hellfire in which masturbation and dirty thoughts are bound to land boy-practitioners of them, there's a moral here.

*   *   *

One more sample, a rather exotic one, of the fertility rite *done live* : this time at the classic junction between White Africa, the sand-coloured lands of the Arabs, and Black Africa, the reptilian green forests of the Negroes—the city where the two Africas meet : Timbuctoo. Little more than a century ago it was the most fabulous city on earth; and even when I first visited it, in 1948, it was still fairly fabulous in the imaginations of most people. Then (but no longer) a remote outpost of the French colonial empire, it had been visited by few Europeans other than a handful of French administrators and soldiers; it still required, if it was to be reached, a hazardous journey across the Sahara desert or from the African west coast across uncharted country with neither roads nor airfields. I went there in 1948 in a friend's bush-hopping single-engined aircraft which landed where it could and picked up gas where luck had it; and returned northwards by truck over the Sahara. Timbuctoo lies a few miles above the most northerly arc of the Niger River—a thousand miles from Dakar on the West Coast, and just twelve-hundred and fifty miles due south of Tangier. Northward from the city runs an infinitude, or so it seems, of sand, the rough growth of thorn-tree and camel-grass becoming ever sparser as the world retreats from the vivifying water of the Niger, rapidly dying as it does so. Here roam the nomad Moors of Mauretania and the Touareg, the "veiled men" of the Sahara. The only living creatures in the central wastes of the desert are these strange roving human beings, and their camels. To the south, the other side of the broad Niger, vast plains of scrubby savannah gradually merge through changing densities of green into the forests and bush of tropical Africa. South of the river is true African country : a multitude of Negro tribes live sedentarily in towns or villages and subsist on tillage and stock-raising. These are two utterly different worlds, north and south of the river—as different in earthly terms as Mars must be from Jupiter—but the two meet and almost mingle in the markets of Timbuctoo.

It's in the market-places that Timbuctoo flowers into a life as gaudy and glowing as a field of vast sunflowers or of many-coloured peonies. In the town's crumbling streets of sand and dusty mud-brick, the people's slinking movement seems almost furtive and ashamed; but in the markets life is triumphant and joyous and intense. These are two market-places : a small one under the shadows of arches and arcades, where African women with skins resembling goldleaf or a veneer of some resinous blood-black lacquer and decked with fantastic coiffures of horns and crinkled plaits, clad like butterflies in "booboos"* of orange and scarlet, yellow and blue, sit squatting on the ground behind the goods they have to sell—meat, fish, herbs, peppers, salt, ostrich feathers, and magic remedies; and the other, the livestock market, a huge arena of trodden dusty earth within a semi-circle, after the rainy season, of the mud-stained swollen waters of the Niger; and given shade round its periphery by the immense spreading foliage of the baobab trees. Under their shadow various African artisans work—the blacksmiths who make swords, saucepans, plough-shares, horseshoes, dentists' pincers, or ladies hairpins, almost while the customers wait : a small boy sitting on the ground keeps the charcoal furnace glowing with a bellows like a toy hand-pump; the hairdressers who work for hours on a lady-client's head which, while its owner lies stretched out in luxurious repose, rests upon the coiffeur's lap, handily for his deft fingers; the saddlers, using green and red leather, brass studs and wooden frames, make camel saddles and all the furniture of desert travel.

I've said above that the two worlds of the two banks of the Niger "almost mingle" in the market-places of Timbuctoo:

*A booboo is a long, loose slipover garment somewhere between a night-shirt and an Anglican surplice.

the two worlds meet for barter and commerce and convenience but come scarcely closer to each other than that. The Arab or the Touareg rides in from the desert with a black African boy behind him on the rump of his camel—but the boy is his "servitor," which is the polite word, conforming with Western morals and reform, for "slave"; the Negro swordsmith politely bargains with a "white" customer from the desert—but he sees him as the son of those murdering marauders from the north who for centuries raided and robbed the black dwellers in the city. What true mingling there has been occurred some four hundred years ago, when an expedition from Marrakech made Timbuctoo a province of the Moroccan empire : today, the leading merchants of the city claim Moroccan descent, but are as black-skinned as their "servitors"—and their intercourse with the camel-riding visitors from the Sahara doesn't run much beyond matters of merchandise or occasionally, perhaps, some question of barter involving a young "servitor," female or even male.

And so, through the hours of the morning and beyond, until the afternoon heat sent everybody to sleep under the baobab trees or some overhanging eaves, the great dusty space of the livestock market, with the cooling glint of water around it, was surging with people and creatures and as noisy as a zoo. Camels sat with their legs doubled under them, endlessly chewing the cud and now and then, as camels do, moaning. Some cow camels had with them calves, white and fluffy as lambs and skipping like puppies on stilts. Sheep and goats lay gasping and stupidly bleating; droves of donkeys trotted on to the scene, herded by a boy jolting on the bony rump of one of them and stark naked although he was of an age when, by "civilized" rules, he should have worn at least a *cache-sexe*. In Timbuctoo the boys—and the girls too—wear nothing at all until they have reached the very verge of puberty : boys already circumcized and girls whose breasts are forming like early fruit go quite naked, and unconscious of being naked, until, just as the first pubic hairs appear, they put on a kind of leathern figleaf, tied round the waist by a string. So the gaily cantering donkey boy, hallooing his drove down to the market, jolts happily barebacked on his animal's rump; and his shining black-brown genitals, like a bunch of balloons in the wind, dance against the donkey's lolloping backbone.

There were, therefore, donkeys in the market-place; donkeys which just endlessly stood, as donkeys do, patiently, simply wagging their ears against the flies. And very often the stallions among them, under the influence of the sun and of those natural and lazy thoughts which must go on between the flicking ears, would languidly extrude (as if the operation were an impersonal one having nothing to do with themselves) an enormous black rubbery penis almost as long as their own hindlegs, a great dingy dangling thing like a truncheon; and every so often, the donkey somnolently blinking against the sunlight, desultorily twitching its ears against the flies, perfunctorily moving its weight from one leg to the other—every so often this pendent slim length of gristle and mystery would be seized by a kind of erectile dynamism and would jerk up like a hammer and rap against its own mother-belly; and then subside, gently, as if withdrawing without regret into reserve. Thus, for the donkeys, and the people busy around them, the days passed in the great market of Timbuctoo.

But on the special morning I'm thinking of, at the end of 1948, I was standing spellbound in the middle of this multifarious market throng, gaping at the rainbow colouring of the garments and the burnished chocolate tones of all these beautiful sculptured faces—as if carved out of the most exquisitely polished mahoganies and ebony; gaping at the slight, slim donkey boys, utterly naked, with loins so slender one could almost encircle them with one's two hands, and joggling brown genitals of which they and the crowd were ingenuously unconscious; at the swirling swaggering movement of innumerable men—Negroes, Moors, Touareg : these last carrying throwing-spears, huge swords like a crusader's, and often guns too; at the huge-bosomed matrons with hair plaited into tails like gazelle's horns and with babies, heads lolling and great gazing black eyes, caught on their backs in a kerchief; gaping at the proud and demurely pubescent girls with charming young rounded breasts; gaping at this intoxicating spectacle, unique, certainly in the whole world—when suddenly one of a string of she-asses was discovered by an adjacent stallion to be in heat. . . .

This jackass quickly kicked away a couple of smaller rivals and, with the field clear for himself, was instantly sniffing hungrily beneath the mare's tail, savouring her piquant femaleness with outstretched neck and wrinkling upperlip—that strange pose of exploration which ruminants, and especially equines, assume. And then he was nibbling at her withers, seizing her, holding her, gripping her neck in his teeth—I suppose it's the asinine ritual rape.

By now a great crowd had formed a circle round the pair of amorous donkeys, as a crowd collects round two men having a fight, or round the victim of an accident; everybody, from any infant who could just walk to one excited ancient who almost couldn't, knew exactly what was about to happen —and everybody was bent on enjoying every moment of it. But it was evident that enjoyment wasn't their only hope : they expected, too, to *profit* from this splendidly public performance. Judging by the enthusiasm and excitement and general approval—the behaviour of people at a circus, also an ancient rite—this gay and applauding congregation of enthusiasts (and, as so many of the faces revealed, worshippers) were making of this simple farmyard copulation a wonderworking fertility rite, done *live* : so much more real than the "harvest festival" of some protestant Christian sect.

The enormous black phallus—asinine proportions are outrageously presumptuous—became distended and imperative beyond description and when its owner, after one or two boss shots, finally mounted satisfactorily there was a general murmur of pleasure and awe—but the women in the encircling crowd bashfully turned their backs, giggling delightedly, beaming all over their broad black faces, and, like women all over the world, pretending they hadn't seen. For in mid-Africa, too, ladylike modesty is the rule; and women avert their eyes from impropriety. But they still relish a good fertility rite, even with their backs to it.

The she-ass stood like one that really wanted it; and the stallion had no bother once he was in : his forelegs fondly clasping his mate's ribs, he rode her like a jockey sure of his mount; thrusting and screwing and playing her as a trombonist plays his instrument. The crowd gaped : their huge blue-white eyes with fiery black irises moist with awe; and when the jackass, after making his final triumphant thrust, at last let his forequarters drop to the ground, the crowd uttered a kind of whispered gasp, a huge unanimous sigh of fulfilment. And there he stood, just behind his ladylove, looking slightly foolish with his head rather drowsily nodding; while his dangling black penis, though now visibly retreating, was still expending a thin albescent dribble. And everybody was happy : the grown-ups were slapping each other on the back and grinning with the pleasure of people who've been told good news; and young people were jumping and skipping with excitement; and the ladies, with their backs turned, were smiling with a snug, ladylike contentment.

I had witnessed a fertility rite, *done live*.

*   *   *

Walking away, pensive after so solemn and yet so boisterous an event, I found myself beside a tall, lean youth with a friendly air and wearing a booboo of sky-blue, faded from much washing. His skin was fair for an African of this part of the Niger : I guessed he might be a Bambara from the Bamako region, five hundred miles upriver, who are generally lighter in colour than the Songhai of the country about Timbuctoo—but what I principally noticed at the time was how prettily his complexion, which was something the colour of a walnut, accorded with the blue of his shirt. A string round his neck held a red leather pouch, about the size of a cigarette-lighter, which must have contained some *gri-gri,* a protective charm. His large horny feet were bare, and flat-soled from fifteen years of walking bare—that was what I judged his age to be by the indices of height, appearance, and so on; but he may have been thirteen, for all I ever discovered —or seventeen.

"*Joli beaucoup,*" he said to me conversationally, jerking his fine round head backwards towards the donkeys. Certainly, I agreed, "*très joli.*"

"*Beaucoup joli,*" he affirmed, as if re-ordering his words must give them added weight. "*Oui,*" I agreed.

"*Bon beaucoup ça,*" he went on, "*beaucoup bon.*"

I thought at first, as a seasoned old European would, that these conversational openings were a deliberately provocative ploy; but later I found they weren't that at all—he was merely commenting, in the only French he knew, on what was, to him, an important and, he hoped, auspicious happening. And I found that the word *beacoup,* joined now and then with a few other words to vary the meaning, was the fulcrum of his French and from it our conversation worked—fortunately he knew also a few words like *bon* and *joli* which sometimes came in useful.

We walked together; and I asked him his name. It was Moossa or Musa, the Arabic form of Moses, so I knew he was a Muslim (since the sixteenth-century Moorish incursion into the whole region of northern Niger, most of the inhabitants have been Mohammedanized—as are, of course, the Mauretanians of the Sahara and, in a delightfully vague, heretical way, the Touareg). Musa continued through the dust by my side; he appeared to take it for granted, though nothing whatever had been said (what could be said with *"beaucoup"*?), that he should continue. And, for myself—well, Musa was an agreeable, friendly creature.

I was staying on the top floor of a solid, rather grandiose house let me by one of the rich men of the town—there were a dozen, perhaps, who owned the city's real estate among them. He was a nice man who kept a huge store : imported European textiles are the things to sell to the people; gold comes up from the south, and glittering rock salt, of great value (it's been legal currency in Timbuctoo), from the north. He was a pleasant, middle-youngish, bearded man, shrewd as a man can be, who dressed more "Moorish" than African and called himself a Moroccan. He invited me to see his daughter preparing for her wedding : and there she lay, prone on the floor of his house, while every kind of practitioner tended her hair and her clothes and her person, making her beautiful.

So Musa came with me to my lodging, which adjoined a large *terrasse* open to the sky from whose walls one could look over Timbuctoo in all directions—and what's almost as important, it included a bog (how the sanitary system of Timbuctoo worked I don't think I ever discovered, but it *did* work) and a glorious well-head where one could draw up, from some subterranean stream, buckets unendingly of lovely cool water (anything cool was difficult to find in Timbuctoo).

But Musa had no idea of staying the night; he had a home, and he went there, I suppose, every evening; but he was back before dawn—he used to shake me awake—to say that everything was *"beaucop bon."* Musa adopted me, for the whole of the daylit hours. He appointed himself my protector and my guide.

It's very hot in Timbuctoo, and an almost hourly duty I gave to Musa once I realized he'd come to stay was to haul up bucket after bucket of water from our well and pour it over me—and then he caught the habit; and so, on our flat roof, we were both scampering stark naked over our *terrasse* and taking turns to haul buckets up from the depths and throw the water over each other. Fortunately the house was taller than its neighbours, so there was nobody to watch our nudist antics.

And nobody to see Musa's surprising possession; in all my life, throughout which I've seen a good many, I'm sure I've never seen as big a one on anybody—of any race and any age. Musa was aware that he possessed something exceptional; he would pick it up and allow its length to droop over the palm of his hand, as if showing an eel he had just caught. *"Joli beaucoup, ça—oui? Beaucoup joli?"* he would say— and this display wasn't intended to provoke; it was just a matter of personal pride in what was, after all, a collector's piece : like somebody showing off his Picasso.

He was proud of it; but wasn't in the least interested in doing anything with it—that is, he didn't reveal in my presence any interest. I never saw him show the slightest sign of sexual curiosity—and certainly never with even the beginning of an erection. He would simply lift it up and weigh it in his hand, like one of those gardening experts evaluating a vegetable-marrow : *"Joli beaucoup, oui?"* he would grin rather sheepishly, his big dark mouth opening on a glint of exquisite animal teeth. He was a plain boy really—plain in the sense that his undistinguished African features, charming now because they were young, rarely reflected anything of humour or animation behind them. I used to suspect, though without any evidence, that he would now and then take the small pocket-money I gave him, along with his enormous possession, to Timbuctoo's single *maison tolérée,* the city's very modest brothel which contained a couple of women. Musa never talked of any girlfriend. But surely he must have done *something*?

It wasn't Musa who asked me if I should like to buy a small girl and take her away with me. I think it was the landlord of my house : that large, stately, genially patronizing magnate, whose coal-black African dignity was enhanced by the Moroccan manners and garb he wore. "I can let you have a nice girl of ten, eleven, very cheap, very hard-working. Your wife—"he assumed of course that I must have a wife in my country—"your wife will train her easily for housework." I was very attracted by the idea of buying a little-girl slave—I hadn't yet been offered a boy-slave—but I could see that in these days of air travel, passports, and immigration police, it might be difficult to carry her around the world. In fact, I don't think he can have made the offer in all seriousness : in 1948 and 1949 a domestic form of slavery certainly existed in Timbuctoo : the rich families had servants who had been born into the household in bondage—and who, to my knowledge, would have been appalled by any thought of being "freed" by their employers, or owners; and in the Desert the "noble" Touareg possessed their *bellah*—the black African "servitors" who were born into the service of their camel-raising nomad masters. Slavery, indeed, was illegal under the French law which in 1948 ruled in those regions : the word *esclave* had been changed to *serviteur*—from "slave" to "servant."

So there was nothing whatever sexual in my relations with Musa—at least not from his side; from mine, I enjoyed immensely—and there was sexual emotion in my enjoyment—those rooftop sessions with the watering-can : I loved watching the miraculous movements of his lithe young body : tall, elegantly slender; with all those perfectly attuned sinews and muscles working like music beneath the walnut-brown skin. He had, topped by this rather dull, yet endearing face, one of the loveliest bodies, and most graceful limbs, I've ever seen : Praxiteles would have carved him over and over again.

And, to my delight and tantalization, he had this prodigious phallus : the moment he took his booboo off, slipping it over his shoulders, I was fascinated, mesmerised, bemused—and who, I wonder, wouldn't have been : for the great god Pan, and the eternal procreator Priapus, still hold sway, even over those who've never heard of them.

We went bathing in the lagoon, made by the flood waters

of the rainy season, near the cattle-market; and sometimes the nine miles or so down to the River Niger itself, and swam in its muddy, fish-filled waters—here human traffic was too noisy for crocodile or hippopotamus. We went northwards, as guests of the French Army, into the confines of the true Sahara; and ate gazelle meat for supper and saw the strings of wild ostriches, like long-distance runners, trotting over the desert.

And he showed me all there was to see of the town: it's hardly a show-place among cities. The two fabulous mosques, with pinnacled towers like huge slabs of gingerbread cake, spiked all over with protruding poles, reminded me of those puddings of my childhood which were prickly with angelica. The streets were floored with thick dusty sand; the houses, built of impermanent bricks pervious to all the elements, were forever crumbling and forever being bolstered up; it was a city, millenially ephemeral and inveterately renascent, built upon sand—and, on the whole, in spite of the candescent sky and the yellow-white sand on which it stood, gloomy and overcast by an air of decay. The cheeriest sight in the streets, apart from most people's gay apparel, was the groups of schoolboys, sitting in the dust, each boy with his huge black writing board: sometimes a schoolmaster would appear to give them a Koranic lesson in the street.

And then I had to go, as in this life one always has to go: and the moment came when I had to say goodbye to Musa. Because I'm very bad at saying goodbye in a sensible, un-emotional way to people I'm fond of, I said goodbye to him in the dust, outside my front door. I took his calm drooping brown hand, with its long beautiful fingers and uncut nails, and shoved a modest little packet of French currency into it. He looked at the banknotes casually and looked up at me. Then he looked down at the money in his hand again. *"Joli beaucoup ça,"* he said.

CATANIA

WERE A trophy to be offered for competition among all the municipalities of the world for the most unabashed, ingenuous and confiding display, open to the public gaze, of juvenile eroticism, I believe it would be easily won by the city of Catania, on the eastern shore of Sicily. There, in a certain part of the city seaboard, a boy will as unblushingly jerk himself off as a horse will lift its tail and unburden its bowels. One knows, of course, that the healthy-minded people of Italy in general, and in southern Italy especially, have little comprehension of the conventional north-European pruderies—one knows that they don't blanch at the thought of crapping in public or feel faint when a gust on a windy beach blows up their shirt and reveals everything beneath; nor are the young of Italy, as a rule, shy of showing the passer-by all they've got. But the boys at Catania must surely take the cake for the unashamed tirelessness of their interest in their sexual powers. In that part of the town which I'll shortly describe, a kind of marathon of masturbation seems to be in unflagging progress, as if the moment one youth has finished another takes up the flaming torch, in order to keep the thing going all round the clock. It's some eleven years since I was in Catania and all this may have changed : that angle of the shore between harbour and beach may, for all I know, have been built over with dance-halls and discothèques and all the refinements of the commercialised lido, and that long line of noble rocks below the harbour wall may have been turned into a neon-lighted promenade—but if these things have happened, then I'll bet the boys have found some other theatre for their pranks.

One wonders what was the genetic source of this specially lubricious exuberance which Catania, more than elsewhere, seems to enjoy? The early Greeks and the much more recent Spaniards are the two foreign races which the longest politically dominated the town and thus most noticeably left their imprint, cultural and physical, upon the natives. Or what of the pre-historic Sikuls, who must be the ultimate ancestors of today's citizens—anyhow this side of the gods? Can the proximity of Mount Etna, against whose nethermost skirts Catania nestles, with her constant volcanic smoking and fuming and rumbling, her frequent eruptions of flame and vapour and glowing hot rock, and her periodical engulfment of every town within reach beneath the molten lava of her vomit—can Etna's constant and godlike menace have caused such nervous tension or psychological disturbance to those old superstitious Sikuls that the only relief they could find was in repeated sexual distraction?

If, walking down the Via Etnea, you stop for a moment and look back, you will see the immense grey-green backcloth of Etna's lowest slopes. But Etna herself you won't see: you're too close up against her base, and you'll know nothing of her everlasting breath-taking surge upwards, far beyond the mere magnitudes of Sicily's dizziest heights—for that you want to be twenty or a hundred miles away. From the Via Etnea it's like trying to look at a colossal statue of Antinous from beside its feet, and seeing nothing above the knees.

At the bottom of this main street you pass the great baroque cathedral which replaced the great Norman pile destroyed in the earthquake of 1693, and also the famous elephant made of lava, a touristical lure prominent in all the travel agents' brochures. Beyond the railway arch, which takes you into the fish-market and past a tiny garden of near-tropical shrubs, leave for another time the turning to the right which leads to the mighty Castello Ursino built in the 13th century by *stupor mundi*, the "wonder of the world" (there are many things to be seen in Catania besides the segment of the seashore to which I'm now directing you); keep straight on along the broad and rather squalid thoroughfare which skirts on its left the boundary of the *porto vecchio*, the old harbour, and suddenly you will come to the open sea, and a broad littoral of clean fine sand shelving gently to the water and stretching infinitely into the southern distance with a range of tree-shadowed dunes along its landward edge. You have arrived.

To the left, at right-angles to the road, there runs out into the sea for a quarter of a mile or so a massive reef of rock, reinforced here and there by huge cubes of concrete, forming a natural breakwater and the bedrock for the high southern wall enclosing the harbour basin. The rocky reef is of great importance : it's the real goal of your expedition, though the spacious expanse of beach between it and the nearest of the wooden structures used by fishermen and, after mid-June, the official bathing establishments, will generally reward some time spent idling upon it. For this stretch of sand is at most times totally unmarked by the print of human feet—except for those of the boys who in fine weather come there in pursuit of their own pleasures.

The road which passes this part of the shore is raised upon an embankment well above the dunes below that fringe of the beach itself; a low wall runs along its edge, on which one may comfortably lean while making a preliminary survey of any gambollers among the sands there may be. At the corner of the harbour wall, one may either walk expectantly along the path above the rocks (one never knows what one may find among them), a path flattened and polished by the happy feet of centuries of boyhood—rarely do people other than boys use it, for it leads nowhere—or one may scramble down over the boulders on to the beach itself, upon which, if the sun's already hot enough to be felt on the skin, there are pretty sure to be a few naked figures playing at the water's edge or stretched dreaming on the sand.

A word of warning here about *season,* to the visitor who comes to Catania for this special purpose. Before April, at the earliest, no nudity will be found here (though even in winter one may chance upon a stray reveller among the secrecies of those rocks); and from the beginning of June the odious rash, endemic nowadays on every discoverable beach, of striped umbrellas, transistor radios, and the sexual simperings of semi-clad female exhibitionists, begins to show—by midsummer's day the beach has become a full-blown "resort." But through April and May it is empty of adults, except for a handful of fishermen who are interested in nobody's business but their own; and in some years, though not in many, the April sun can be as powerful as June's. And it's the sun that brings the boys out: anywhere in southern Italy, when the sea is near, the tingle of real heat on their skins will have their clothes off and themselves into the water even if it's a sham summer— I've seen boys swimming in Palermo harbour on New Year's Day.

This was a very wide beach; in some parts, the water's edge was as much as three or four hundred yards from the road and the nearest areas of villadom: too far to excite the interest of policemen or old ladies or anyone who felt keenly about the public decencies; while the wooden structures, raised from the sand on piers, of the summer-season bathing establishments were empty and unattended and provided excellent theatres for all sorts of games. So no bathers bothered, during the month of May or in April when the sun was hot enough, about swimming costumes; and on a flaming day the surf would be twinkling with a galaxy of naked boys' bodies, and the sand dancing with them like a netful of jumping fish just landed. A favourite pastime, and perhaps a tradition, was the scooping out of the sand of a trough about the size of a coffin—long enough to allow its scooper to lie in it full-length and deep enough to keep him below the horizon of wanderers upon the beach, at least until they were right on top of him. Sometimes two friends would construct such a tomb of a width to contain them both, though tightly packed; sometimes they'd dig two side by side, so that while solitarily working away at themselves they were still within conversing distance of each other. On a really hot day, when the boys from the neighbouring tenements and slum streets around the old Swabian castle flocked to the sea like a drove of thirsty fauns making for a river, one would find two or three of them snuggling together inside almost any of the fishermen's boats which had been hauled ashore and temporarily left idle by its owner; while an expanse of rolling dunes, a range of Saharan hills in miniature, into which one part of the upper beach merged, generally concealed in its hollows a few youngsters of various ages from ten upwards intent upon some sort of mutual pleasure. The boys on this beach were nearly always entirely content with their own or each other's company—they weren't looking for help from strangers and they didn't at all encourage any intrusion.

That line of rocks, however, below the harbour wall was rather different. Here also the boys came in hot weather, singly or in pairs or in gangs of three to a dozen, to bathe and sprawl naked on their favourite slabs of boulder, and to play with themselves luxuriously in the many small caverns and gullies among the rocks that seemed specially built for this purpose. But here there came too a few knowing youths who kept a lookout for any patrolling queers who might find their way to this out-of-the-way spot, and often their time wasn't wasted: an adventurous tourist might be roped in; and there were two or three Italian regulars. These speculative lads, missing no chance, would plant themselves in view of any likely looking man who appeared on the rocks and, with an air of careless indifference, would take off their clothes and arouse themselves into a most provocative sexual condition and simulate a state of intense desire; the man, if he didn't take offence, would fall helplessly into the trap, which would cost him more money than he expected before the day was out.

But most of the boys who played in the sunshine on these brown and tawny rocks paid attention to nobody but themselves or their friends. They came simply to amuse themselves in the pleasantest and most natural way known to them, when it was too hot for the cinema and anyhow they had no money. Sunday morning, I found was an especially busy time on the rocks: they trooped down saunteringly in dozens—mostly boys of fifteen or sixteen, who had finished with school and were working through the week: they came for their weekly swim, and their Sunday morning wank in the serene and carefree conditions of uninhibited nakedness which this shore allowed. Most of them seemed to have a favourite spot to which their languid, contented footsteps led them as if from long habit—some special gully between two high boulders: a vaulted cavern that chance or geology had built beneath the roof of the rocks; or a long, flat, sloping boulder, suitably tilted for the sun and a view of any splashing friends in the sea; and one party of four, I remember, seemed almost to have taken the lease of a capacious ledge which, shielded from prying eyes above by a high and unscaleable reredos of rock, offered a perfect board from which to dive or platform on which to recline : the four lessees of this delightful perch (their squatting rights seemed to be recognized by the other regulars of the rocks) came every Sunday morning and always together —they were plainly what British boys call "mates." They all four looked about fourteen or fifteen; to reach their ledge they squeezed down through a gap between two boulders and followed a tortuous kind of gallery below—no stray wanderer above would spot this secret passage (I one day was specially privileged). Between them they brought two or three long loaves stuffed with tomato (or, when they were lucky, with *mortadella*), and a bottle or two of some fizzy drink; and, after a quick swim, they would lie together on the flat warm stone, drying in the fierce sun and idly commencing the earliest processes of their Sunday morning masturbation; now and then pausing to compare notes or to ask each other what progress was being made. . . .

I made no friends while I was in Catania : only two or three acquaintances, whose specious cordiality generally was intertwined with financial requirements that weren't fun at all. It didn't strike me as a good town for friends; but it was a wonderful place for sights to see. . . .

But all this happened a decade or more ago. Everything may be different now : the very geography of that shore and harbour wall may have changed. Yet the boys of Catania won't have changed, apart from the imperceptible gliding of the generations one into the other. Boys, I think, never change.

DAKAR

It was in Dakar that I respectfully declined an invitation to dine with the Governor-General of French West Africa because I had a date with a barefooted black boy who had picked me up the night before.

This must have been about 1949; and the Place Protet, the wide square pleasantly shaded by palm trees where I'd met him, hadn't yet earned its present name of "Place de l'Indépendence" : Dakar was still the administrative capital not only of Senegal but also of a number of vast tribal territories which today are sovereign nations. The French still ruled; and Dakar was already the "gay" city of West Africa; when I returned nine years later, the French rulers had gone; and Dakar was gayer than ever.

I suppose this sad yet bubblingly cheerful waif was about fourteen years old. He had, I remember—seeing in my expression friendliness and probably, too, invitation—rushed over and flung his long thin arms round me, pressing his naked dusty-black chest against me and saying a lot of what I hoped were African endearments. He was wearing nothing but an African variety of sarong, and a smile that made his plain, flat, fleshy face wonderfully beautiful.

In fact, it was lucky for me that the gubernatorial dinner-party happened that night, because the two friends I was travelling with went to it and spent the evening in grand and rather stuffy company, while I had to myself the flat the three of us had been lent. To myself, that is, and the black boy I believe I enjoyed my evening better than they enjoyed theirs. Even now, twenty years later, I can still see in my mind the gentle lines of that lean—yet so loving—ebony body and remember the clinging of his limbs. The very sparkle of his nature, the very warmth of his response, enhanced his pathos, the desperate sadness of the young life ahead of him. Scarcely out of his childhood—from all I could make out of his touching chatter—he was on his own : of family, he knew none; if there were any government or charitable institutions looking for him and his like, he carefully eluded them—with that natural instinct which prizes liberty above everything else. He earned what centimes he could as a part-time shoeblack—and God knows there are too many shoe-blacks in Dakar : each pavement café has its "official" team of half-a-dozen or more shoeshine boys who squat on the pavement-edge with their wooden boxes of pads and brushes, quarrelling and joking over each newly arrived customer, flashing their huge white eyes around the people sitting at the tables, and exchanging an endless backchat of jolly obscenities —an anarchical, ebullient company of charmingly-mannered bandits whose only cares were hunger and which doorstep to sleep on tonight. What chance could there be for a part-timer?

Dakar at that time, except for the grandiose administrative palaces of the French Government and their social equals, the commercial edifices of the great French firms which made their fortunes out of products like peanut oil and phosphates, seemed to be a sprawling maze of African huts and shanty-town suburbs—*"bidonvilles"* is the nice French word for them—from whose walls rows of repulsive baldheaded vultures gazed down on the lookout for offal. When I saw Dakar again nine years later, the administrative centre seemed merely a subsection of a great modern city; the population had grown to something like a quarter of a million people; and there were more shoeshine boys than ever. . . .

*   *   *

Anybody who's read my account earlier in this book of some experiences in Timbuctoo will have perceived that it couldn't be advertised as "gay." Dakar, however, one thousand miles to the west, on the Atlantic coast, certainly can. Two over-simple reasons, perhaps, occur to one in explanation of this : it's been one of the great West Coast ports of call for European and American shipping during two or three centuries, and an entrepôt of foreign commerce, and its people thus have learned a lot about how to provide "white" needs; and two hundred years ago Dakar was one of the main ports loading slaves for the Caribbean sugar plantations and the cotton fields of the southern States : the unhappy natives of Dakar learned a thing or two in those days.

But that's not all there is to it : for some reason, buried in history and ethnography, the Senegalese—the people who inhabit the vast plains on either side of the Senegal river, raising livestock and harvesting the easy-growing peanut— have a reputation in all those regions for homosexuality, and in Dakar one may quickly see that they merit this reputation.

Why, I've often wondered, isn't homosexuality rife, or at least noticeable, in Timbuctoo also? One would think that a populace subject so long to the influence and often to the rule of the men of the desert would have become accustomed to desert habits. But, then, is homosexuality a Touareg habit or propensity? I doubt it, though it may sometimes provide a diversion : the Touareg, in their caravans, lug their huge fleshy women with them astride their camels (to the Touareg noble's eye, female obesity equals allure). It's likely to be a traditional mode of pleasure among the swarthy nomad Moors of the southern Sahara; but these, though they are in and out of Timbuctoo to barter supplies or have their saddlery or weapons seen to, have never dominated the city's people and never stay there. And when I knew Timbuctoo the boys there were so unused to white visitors who even *noticed* them, that they shied away from any approach—not from fear of sexual assault but from plain shyness. As late as 1958, there wasn't much sign, that I could see, of queerness in Timbuctoo. But in Dakar !

*   *   *

The whole matter should be so interesting to an anthropologist, and is so puzzling to the mere uninstructed observer that one may insert a brief note—for the sake of readers who don't know the country—about the surprisingly sharp differences between the Senegalese and the people of Timbuctoo. The ordinary American and European who doesn't know about Africa thinks that it's all the same—just Africans, looking the same, coloured the same, speaking the same. This, of course, is nonsense.

For example, a young man from Dakar, a Senegalese, who had come to Timbuctoo as one of our party, started questioning some "locals" one day when we were walking through the market. He was furious when they didn't understand him —and he couldn't understand them. *"Sont des idiots, quoi?"* he exclaimed irritably; *"Sont des indigènes, ces types-là?"* "They're just a lot of natives, these idiots." And, of course, that's just what the people of Timbuctoo thought about any other "foreigners" whose language they didn't know, black though their skins might be.

Dakar has no real ethnic affinity with Timbuctoo, apart from all being African together; nor really any geographical —the vast stretches of Africa which the great windings of the Senegal river kept alive are utterly different from those that the fabulous Niger nourish—though on the map their two tails are tantalizingly close. Half a dozen languages are spoken in the varying tribal territories between Dakar and Timbuctoo; the architecture of the beautiful mud-brick buildings one sees in any of the few large villages along the route, keeps changing in a dramatic way that shows a change in communal need and idea; colour alters too : the people of Senegal are generally lighter than the people of Africa further south; they are, might one say, the colour of coffee with a little cream in it. But once you get beyond the source of the Senegal, and far beyond the source of the young Niger, you suddenly find the people lighter still : the colour perhaps of a very dark local English cheese; and now the country is the sovereign republic of Mali—it's the heir to one of the great Niger empires of that name and today includes Timbuctoo. But the people around Timbuctoo are, again, much darker : they are Songhai. Dakar knows nothing of all that : the name "Timbuctoo" is better known in the nurseries of Europe than in the neon-lit bars of up-to-date Dakar.

The Dakar of 1958 was the Paris of Africa. The French, in their old colonial days, possessed a genius for evoking the atmosphere of *la métropole,* as they called metropolitan France, wherever they settled down and whomever they settled among : as they did in Saigon and Hanoi, in Indochina; as they did in the towns of Arab North Africa; as they did in Djibouti, capital of the French slice of Somaliland; and as they most certainly did throughout their dominions in West and Equatorial Africa—and nowhere more enduringly than in Dakar. In 1958 Senegal had just become an independent republic; but French was still the administrative language, and in any of Dakar's bars and cafés one could easily, if one closed one's mind to the climate and the predominance of black skins, suppose oneself in Paris.

*   *   *

That one didn't have to be shy in Dakar, and even less furtive, if one was queer became pretty plain to me almost my first evening there (I'm writing now of my second visit). I was in a rather low bar, just off the city's principal boulevard and in the heart of the French quarter. The woman behind the bar, obviously the proprietress, was a typical big-bosomed colonial Frenchwoman; a few men, whites, were sitting with a typically French-colonial moroseness in front of their *apéritifs,* waiting for God knows what—probably their return to *la métropole*; a couple of European tarts, blonde, brash and brassy and no longer in their first youth, were making up their faces in a corner and gossiping—it was early yet for customers: these morose males were clearly putting off the moment when they must go back to their wives.

And suddenly, into this typically small-town ambience of the French provinces, there swished a middle-aged *tapette* with an ebony skin, orange silk bellbottoms, a sky-blue satin blouse and dangling gold earrings—and this was some ten years before our male sartorial revolution in Europe and America. He seemed about the campest thing I've ever seen : the featherweight lithe figure of a boy-dancer, the giggles and lisps and little shrieks, as he toyed with his *bock* of pale beer, of a coquettish schoolgirl, and the wrinkles and ogling knowingness of an ageing queen. Obviously there were no customers for him in this bar—the few Frenchmen on their bar-stools still gazed sadly into their glasses, apparently unaware of this sudden shrill presence. The *patronne* served him his beer and took his money, and exchanged with him the usual pleasantries of the evening; to her he was a customer : for any Frenchwoman who sits at the till, it's the till that makes the social rules.

But the two tarts in the corner owned quite a different sort of till. The moment the queen swished in, they dropped their gossip and their face-making and got their weapons ready; by the time he was half way through his *bock*, they attacked: they launched one of those battles of abuse which French tarts generally win.

But their abuse wasn't directed at his being gay, at his being a queen, at his sexual morality or his sexual practice, nor at his colour—they abused him simply because, so they alleged, he was trespassing in their beat.

"You and your kind," they said to him, "you're taking a living away from honest girls like us. Can't you go somewhere else—can't you go to your own bars? Why've you got to spoil our trade? You're just a lousy spoil-trade, that's what you are." They spoke in what one might call *dakarois*—a local slang-French interlaced with plenty of African slang-words, or rather words made slang by the French. What impressed me was their evident and uncritical acceptance of what he *was*— just as one would accept somebody's being a wigmaker or a Jehovah's Witness: that's the sort of chap he is, one would say, and leave it at that. It was intrusion into their territory that the tarts were angry about; they seemed to think that this fifty-year old queen, which is what I judged his age, really did mean a competition in their own trade. Right through this discussion, the *patronne* sat omnisciently beside her till; one by one the men lowered themselves from their inelegant perches, primed at last to return to their homes. They seemed not to have noticed that there'd been any altecation in the bar. When I left, the tarts and the queen were still there: customers for all would doubtless arrive later. The *patronne* remained by the till.

Further evidence of Dakar's atmosphere of permissiveness, of the moral indifference with which other people's private diversions seemed generally to be regarded, cropped up in the small hotel where I was staying. It was French-owned; and characteristic of hundreds of its kind to be found wherever the French are: cheap, clean and uncomfortable—and, of course, the inevitable Cerberus in the hall, controlling every visitor's entry and exit. The rooms were tiny, each with its own shower, and the beds were enveloped in a tent of mosquito-netting. Sometimes the Cerberus was an agreeable Senegalese hall-porter; sometimes Madame herself guarded the stone stairway leading up to the rooms: anybody who went up or down those stairs was observed. When, therefore, I wanted to bring a young African in his early teens to my room—a shoeshine boy who in his ragged singlet and shorts looked as if he badly needed the shower-bath he was coming to enjoy—I knew there wasn't a hope of smuggling him in. So I walked boldly in, followed by my barefooted guest, and, finding Madame on guard, called out gaily "bonjour, Madame," with all the self-assured courtesy I could muster, and made resolutely for the stairs. "Bonjour, M'sieur," she calmly replied, hardly looking up from her account book. . . .

After that my little shoeblack came in and out unquestioned —and he wasn't the only one either.

*　　　*　　　*

I'd been introduced to an official of some sort in one of the Ministries : a middle-aged Senegalese of great charm and culture—and himself a lover of boys. Would I care to see a very special side of Dakar night-life, off the regular beat of most foreign visitors to the city? And so one night after dinner—it must have been towards ten o'clock—we set off in his car for some outlying suburb. We soon left the "modern" town behind; and drove through miles of dimly lighted districts of the *"ville indigène"*—long acres of "native quarters" : low-walled cantonments containing, according to tribal customs, either thatched beehive huts or parallelograms of one-room dwellings built of sunbaked brick. Then we came into a world of *bidonvilles*—a twilit, dismal shantytown, constructed of corrugated iron and empty oildrums and any sort of do-it-yourself material that the owner-builder could lay his hands on. From the endless rows of dark and unwelcoming hutments there came a low muttering of human life—the life of the crowded families that lived in them; and, here and there, the throbbing of some deep-voiced drum, beating for a wedding or other family festival. But there was nothing festive in the aspect of these sad districts : behind the general air of squalor and dejection, I got an impression of latent hostility and watchfulness : a notion that all these sullen shells which were the scene of human love and passion and family devotion were on the defensive, on the lookout, in a state of mental siege. That sort of peripheral slum always attracts police interference, to say nothing of those little governmental busybodies

obsessed with things like rates and taxes. . . . The misery of
these acres of human degradation was the product of the
people who suffered it—they need never have come there :
the old, old story of a proud and dignified peasantry lured
from their villages by the glitter of industry and the city. Thus
we move forward towards the golden age.

Somewhere near the core, it seemed, of this labyrinth of
sad—and even a little sinister—dreariness, my friend stopped
his car and said : "Here we are. There are a couple of places
we can look at here—I think you'll see something to amuse
you. . . ."

He parked the car and locked it, and I got out and stood
in the sultry, near-tropical night; and suddenly found that I
was listening to the muffled rhythms of some kind of dance
music : there were drums of course, there are always drums in
Africa, and I love drums; but I also heard the nasal noise of
something like a saxophone, an instrument which has always
seemed to me to emit the opposite of musicality. I began to
wonder where on earth I was being taken to : not surely to
just a night spot. . . .

Fairly full of misgivings, what with the rather weird surroundings, now almost pitch dark, and the saxophone, I followed my guide along a number of narrow and unlit alley-
ways, branching off abruptly at right angles, one way or the
other; till suddenly he stopped at a wooden door at the end of
a blind-alley—and now, all at once, I became aware of a
large arc of illumination being thrown into the night from
whatever might be beyond the door.

The door was opened; my friend talked to somebody or
other—whether it was a club with an entrance fee I can't now
remember; and then we were let in, and walked across what
was an open-air dance-floor of polished and hard-trodden
earth, veneered and admirably dressed with cattle dung, and
found a table : handily adjacent to the door whence the
drinks came and as far as possible from the saxophone. We
sat down, ordered some beer, and looked around. Couples
were dancing, vaguely European dances—after all, Europeans had been dancing, in Dakar, among their other European activities, for two or three hundred years; people were
sitting in tables round the dance-floor in twos and threes—
and a few in solitary expectance. The whole small circular

arena was brightly lit. Our beer was brought—and by now I was really looking around.

The place was full of adolescent Africans in drag.

In drag. I mean that most of them were indeed in girls' clothes—some in European, some wearing the elaborate headdress of the West African mode * —it was in fact a drag party; and, apart from ourselves and perhaps two or three African onlookers of adult age, nobody there, I judged, was more than eighteen years old and most were around fifteen.

They danced together; they camped around like a pride of primadonnas; they came to our table and drank lots of beer with us simpering, blinking their white-powdered eyelids, widening their great carmined lips. Cosmetics—at least the colouring kind—don't suit the African face : the skin anyway is much better protected than is the "white" against the hideosities inflicted by climate or ill health; and perhaps for that very reason makeup produces a bizarre and sometimes an eerie effect when sloshed over an African complexion.

They had pleasant manners, these transvestite Senegalese boys; they were friendly and undemanding, and bubbling with jokes of a tartish kind. They seemed. on the surface, to be as cheerful as boys of that age ought to be. But one couldn't, through all that paint and camp hilarity, see beneath the surface. . . .

We went to a couple of such places; and about midnight drove back to Dakar through the same dark, sinister shantytowns. I went home with what's called a nasty taste in my mouth—not, of course, from any moral biliousness, but because temperamentally I dislike a display of effeminacy in boys and am repelled by an extreme exhibition of it. And also there was the knowledge of the sadness that must lie behind the tinsel—the old sense of tragedy under the clown's greasepaint : although adolescent boys can't often have experienced the feeling of despair, in these pathetic dolled-up tarts despair couldn't be far off.

The most interesting lesson of the evening was that these boy-brothels, for that's what they were (I forgot to ask

*A mode, with the high-waisted booboo, introduced by the fashionable French ladies who, when their husbands colonized Saint-Louis de Senegal in the eighteenth century, made that city almost as elegant as it is today.

whether accommodation could ge got on the premises), hadn't been set up for a special branch of the tourist trade—their remote and dingy situation alone was evidence of that : they were the spontaneous acknowledgement of a native demand, an African taste. For some reason which I don't pretend to know, homosexuality, including the love for adolescent boys, seems to be immeasurably more widely and more convention-ally inveterate among the Senegalese than among any other African people that I have knowledge of.

SOME NOTES ON THE EFFECTS OF "PURDAH" ON BOYS

I HAVE borrowed the word *purdah* from the Indians because it seems to fit what's wanted better than "segregation," which doesn't have quite the right meaning (and now has acquired a new meaning); or "monasticism," which would be right only in some contexts; or "separation of the sexes," which isn't really what happens or what's intended to happen. But the "screening from view" implicit in the word *purdah,* the mental veiling from the idea of intimate contact with the female sex, is what's at the back, I believe (though in quite different ways, and with quite different purposes), of both the British public school system and, say, the strict social taboo in southern Italy on any contact between boys and girls from the age of puberty till, almost, the moment of marriage. What is interesting here, I think, is not the reasons for these customs, nor even their educational merits or demerits—what's interesting is the effect of purdah on the adolescent boy's sexual evolution and sexual habit.

The following notes on this matter come from nothing but my own experience : I try to present facts as I've seen them, or what I've been persuaded are facts, and the consequences that common sense seems able to deduce from them. But I try not to proffer any theories, being incompetent to theorize. All I can do is submit evidence—much no doubt circumstantial—which both sides to the argument may make what they can of.

I have read publications from the United States which reflect the oddest notions of British public schools and what goes on in them : one learns that these boarding schools are, at one and the same time, seminaries for the promotion of a taste for sodomy among Britain's middle-class boyhood, and places where brutal pedagogues, obsessed by sadistic desires, may obtain their sexual satisfaction upon the backsides of pupils whose parents pay about fifteen hundred dollars a year to give them the chance.

I spent, myself, five years in an English public school: in five years one gets some idea of what goes on. I have also, through a number of years after leaving that public school, learned a great deal about the sexual habits of adolescent boys of the British lower class—boys who've never been near a public school and have never been in purdah.

At a British public school, which is a private school, the boy spend some eight or nine months of each of four or five years in purdah: the only females he sees during the three terms, or semesters, are the matron of his "house," the wives of those sadistic schoolmasters, and perhaps some maids—their status at my school is described in our name for them: "skivvies." During the three months of holidays, the boy has all the contact with girls his parents allow him—or what he can snatch despite them.

At a British day school, which generally is a "public" school—that is, a State School—the boys may usually share the buildings with girls and today often share classes too. The boys (and girls) at these schools belong chiefly to the "lower" classes; out of school these boys can have all the contact with girls that home disciplines, which of course vary enormously, and opportunity allow them.

Now what, according to the facts which I've observed during five years at a public school and twice as many years among boys of the working class, are the sexual addictions of these boys; and how, so far as one can judge, have the different systems influenced them?

Let's start with the public school—but sticking to facts, things seen, without trying to explain with the help of theory. At my school, as I believe at most public schools, nakedness was encouraged—I mean we were made to see each other naked, we bathed together naked, swimming in the pool and river was naked: this was a part of the "muscular Christian" theory—a healthy mind in a healthy body (educationists go in a lot for theories)—that if you are accustomed to the sight of the body unashamed you too will be unashamed, and you won't have any dirty thoughts. (There is, of course, some truth in this theory; but only some. In the dormitory, too, there was an emphasis on "non-shame," if one may call it that; under each boy's bed was a pisspot which, according with school custom, was used unashamedly in full view of everybody. There were no doors, throughout the school, on the bogs: the most timid and sensitive mother's darling, almost straight from the nursery, was compelled to crap in inelegant dejection in front of a mob of his mocking fellows.

All this was part of the authorities' technique for keeping the boys uninterested in their own or other people's bodies. They might just as successfully have thought up ways of keeping boys uninterested in food. The boys were permanently interested in their own bodies; quite a number of them were interested in other boys' bodies. Masturbation was done as naturally as it always has been and always will be—it was done in bed in the dorm or in the lavatory or—especially when it was part of a love affair—in the woods and over the downs. The school authorities liked to think that masturbation was "bad form" in the school; now and then they gave little cosy talks about "self-pollution" and even hinted, shame on them, that if we did it a lot we might lose, not merely Christian salvation, but even the sight of our eyes. But beyond masturbation ("rubbing up" it was called at my school), done alone or *à deux* or, now and then in the dorm, in a sort of olympic competition—with laurels for the first or the most; beyond this ordinary schoolboy pleasure, which nobody (except the schoolmasters) thought of much importance, there was a great deal of emotional homosexuality—bigger boys "in love" (yet why put it in inverted commas? It was *love*!) with the unapproachable younger. In these schools there are un-scalable barriers between boys of seventeen and boys of sixteen or fifteen, boys in one House and boys of another: the whole social structure of the school is designed to prevent emotional "contacts" ever contacting. And yet, some impud-ently logical objectors might say, you put these boys in purdah from the female sex and yet ferociously try to suppress (or, conveniently, evade) any emotional—let alone physical—sexuality with their own sex. So love affairs are the natural rule throughout the term; masturbation as ordinary a thing as going to bed. What I never heard of in all the five years

I spent at my public school was buggery. There was plenty of opportunity : although the boys at my school slept together, ten or more in a dormitory, the bigger boys had their "studies" which gave them privacy and had power over "underschool" fags whom they could summon. Yet I never heard of a go at buggery. I've been told that at Eton, Britain's most expensive public school, where each boy has a room of his own, even the small boys, sodomy was a practice which new arrivals were told by their knowing betters to expect. I don't know; I wasn't at Eton. But I do know from experience that schools of all social sorts, like urban districts, move, in the adolescent world, from one phase or fashion or vogue to another—and I mean by this, too, sexual vogues and fashions. For I've known a London district—just a circle of a few streets—where within the space of five years any boy would be ready to be picked up; and in the next five years that vogue would somehow have died out.

As for the sadistic schoolmasters some American authors have written about, I didn't know any at my school. I was "beaten" once, by a prefect (that is, a senior boy placed in some House authority), for some small offence; it didn't hurt much and I didn't once hear of anybody's being badly hurt by master or prefect. The masters I was taught by, mainly badly taught but pleasantly, were a gentle lot who, I think, can never have heard of "sadism," even if they felt within themselves a flicker of that uncharacteristic desire.

And in the holidays, when we went home, we met and "mixed with" the girls in our families' social circle and, those of us who wanted to, flirted with them; most of us— and I mean adolescents from the public schools between fourteen and seventeen—didn't want to flirt; we were more bored by girls than shy of them after our purdah at school; but purdah hadn't in the least made us anti-girl : the big boys of eighteen or so, the "bloods" at school who were on the point of leaving, were—when they were so inclined—as eager as anybody to flirt and make love—purdah hadn't affected their sexual orientation.

The idea of the public schools, I think, sprang from the charity school endowed in past centuries by princes or religious orders, in which foundling boys and the like were held captive, meagrely fed, clad in a "charity" livery, and straightjacketed into law-abiding Christians. From this early "establishment" mode of "catching them young" and turning out docile proles, there developed the subtler idea of adapting this same training method to the other side of the picture : instead of inculcating the habit of submission, the boarding-school idea was turned to the teaching of the art of subjection —the public school came into being as the only recognized nursery of "leadership." It became the school where the sons of the governing class learned how to retain their governance, and the heirs to social privilege how to preserve their heritage. In the last couple of hundred years a kind of mystique, like an odour of sanctity, accumulated round these schools (whose fees have kept going up and up, in order to preserve them for the class that could afford to pay them). Headmasters of the leading public schools began to receive, as saints do, a halo, the attribute of "great," which gave them rather more cachet than a mere knighthood : newspaper obituaries fawned on the memory of men like "the great Dr. Arnold." And then these "great" men, most of them either crusading Christians or bigoted Hellenists, began to mould the schools they ruled into, on the one hand, a monastic pattern, and on the other, some imitation of what they believed to be a Spartan ideal. Hence the British public schools : places with a bastard ancestry and a prejudiced purpose; places where boys of the ruling class (the class, that is, with enough money to pay the fees) are required to spend five years of their adolescence in a moral regimentation which denies them their sexuality and which while it can't deprive them of their sexual organs, pretends that boys are equipped with these things only for eliminant purposes (when I was at school it was difficult to believe that people like headmasters possessed them at all).

That, roughly is the origin and design of the British public school—though today, in 1968, and for some years back already, its nature is inevitably being modified under the pressure of social change.

These schools, conceived in the minds of the "great" headmasters, are run on a foundation of harsh discipline (partly imposed by rules and the sanctions of physical punishment, but much more cleverly by the hypnotic force of "good form" and "tradition" and "in this House we don't do that"). In the interests of "leadership" some selected big boys (designated "prefects," "monitors," "house-captains" and so on; and raised to a rank of school aristocracy) are given powers, if not of life and death then of body and soul, over certain of the little boys: they can whip small boys accused of some tiny offence—they can almost order small boys to wipe their arses. This, the theory goes, leads to "leadership." But the "great" headmasters, sincerely inspired by their Greco-Christian fallacies, cannot understand that, imprisoned behind the screen of the purdah that is the public school for three months at a time, great hulking hairy lads of eighteen, to say nothing of the less hairy ones of fifteen upwards, have romantic and sexual feelings like anybody else ("great" headmasters often have wives, but they never have sexual feelings—that's part of the great tradition). So when a bigger boy is convicted of having formed a romantic attachment with a younger boy he is, at the worst "expelled," and at the best made wretched for the rest of stay at the school. "Expelled," when I was a boy, meant social ruin—there were no plum jobs in the Establishment for a boy who'd been expelled.

In these schools boys—in ages varying from twelve or thirteen to eighteen or sometimes more, and in numbers from some three hundred to five hundred—are kept in purdah, isolated from the rest of the world, for three months at a time. And yet the "great" headmasters, and their pedagogic lieutenants, always seem taken aback—and above all *hurt*— when any of their pupils are discovered to be sexually alive people. The public-school system places its boys in purdah— but it is itself in purdah: it keeps a rigid screen of academic aloofness between itself and the obvious result of the purdah. The whole system provides opportunity and inspiration for precisely what all its "great" men are dedicated to preventing —any kind of sexual contact, even if only romantic, between an older and a younger boy.

It's very odd. And perhaps it seems odder when one thinks that, until perhaps very recently, out of the entrails of this system came Britain's rulers—not merely in politics but wherever "leadership" mattered. And it's amusing to reflect that the sexual heterodoxies which today would be condemned as outrageous by many of our rulers were, in their youth, among their chief delights.

The British public school system is thus a house divided

against itself—it is devoted to principles which its very structure was designed to deny. On the one hand, the boys it trains to "leadership" are taught that any form of sexuality is at best "bad form" and at worst an unforgiveable evil that must be gouged out of the school's life, whenever it is found, like a weed out of a rose-garden; and on the other, it ensures, by enclosing its pupils in a kind of emotional harem, that a great number of boys around puberty are introduced to some form of homosexual experience—romantic or physical—long before they would have found out about it if they'd been kept in their sheltered homes. On the one hand, it proclaims that a certain plant is poisonous and must never be grown; on the other, its own soil is of such a nature that it inevitably becomes the seedbed of that same plant. A boy arriving at a public school is presented with *opportunities* for homosexual relationships which he'd never have dreamed of at his home—and probably, because of the purdah he's held behind, makes the most of them while he remains there. But that doesn't mean that he'll be homosexual after he leaves his school, no matter how much experience he may've had. If he isn't a homosexual through life, he will after emerging from purdah become respectably "normal" and, like so many leaders of the British establishment, look back upon the unlawful lecheries of his public school as mere boyish pranks.

It's a very odd system which, like so many British institutions, blundered into existence and then found itself the consecrated nursery of privilege and "leadership" in Britain's imperialist century. Today, with the perquisites of empire vanished, privilege open to anybody who can afford to pay a lot for it, and "leadership" becoming more and more a politician's label, the public school doesn't quite know where it's going. It is still, of course, true to type, trying to have things both ways; trying to stay stuck where it was and at the same time move ahead with "progress." The public schools are scratching their heads over the problem of how to mix an educational cocktail of the fee-paying sons of the rich and the State-supported "scholarship boys" of the working class. They have even, in 1968, been presented with the proposal that girls should share the benches and desks of the Sixth Form : where then will purdah be?

There have, of course, for many decades existed some

renowned co-educational schools in Britain : fee-paying, expensive, and very "progressive." Dartington Hall is a famous one; Bertrand Russell's experiments are well-known; and Bedales School is perhaps the oldest and most conventional of them all. One of the principal theories behind these schools is that the free and comradely mingling of the sexes will nurture an emotional normality among their adolescent pupils. Most certainly, and most obviously, this system is more "normal" than the purdah-system of the boys' public school and must avoid much of the sexual vicariousness which such a multitude of public-school boys are required to enact; but it can have little effect—I believe none—upon the ultimate sexual bifurcation of adolescence—each individual somewhere between the ages of fifteen and eighteen moves in the direction which nature has mapped out; and what experiences boys and girls may have had during those years can't alter the destined choice of direction, though they may hasten it.

When I was a boy of seventeen or so, my most pertinaciously homosexual acquaintance of about my own age was a boy at the co-ed school of Bedales—and homosexual he remained, I know, well into his maturity.

But comparatively few boys in Britain spend their five years or so of purdah in the public schools. The huge majority of British boys belong to the working class and the "lower middle class" as it's called; and they go to the State schools, elementary and secondary. Some of the "lower middle-class" boys are sent by the parents, who want to pay to be "posh," to privately owned or subsidized schools—the fact of paying fees, though small ones, confers status. But all these schools, State or fee-paying "private" schools, are *day schools* : that's the point—there's no purdah there : the boys live at home and their association with girls is just as free as they themselves wish and their parents endorse. They live in a world utterly different from the purdah world of the public school boys : they're not enclosed in any monastical exclusiveness, cut off from females for three months at a time : they're at home with all their sisters and cousins and aunts and under the daily care of their mothers and, besides, they've got the run of the streets and of all the girls in the neighbourhood. And what is the sex life of the average London boy of fourteen or fifteen or sixteen?

There was a time, many years ago, when I saw a good deal of it. At that time—say thirty years ago—the ordinary London working class kid's sex life wasn't much different from that of the public school boy's sex life in purdah—although the London street boys played and joked and daily associated with the girls of the neighbourhood. But these boys, whenever they were together in twos or threes or fours in playgrounds or bathing places or, when available, each other's houses, *instantly* and perhaps even more impetuously, started the same masturbatory games as are played in the public schools. Among working-class schoolboys, homosexual acts are commonplace in their daily lives and have little of the portentousness which similar behaviour seems to have in the public schools : free of the mystique of purdah, working-class boys aren't subject to the same taboos. But the homosexual games of working-class boys are less emotional; not being in purdah their romanticism can find ample outlet in the girls they daily see around them—most adolescent kids, probably, enjoy a romantic dream about some girl they come into contact with, while their physical sex they enjoy in the company of their "mates." The romantic need is perhaps felt later in working-class adolescence than in the cloistral life of a public school, which is itself romantic—the whole ambience of the place, with its "gothic" buildings and traditions, artificially promotes a precocious emotionalism and hunger for romantic attachments. Yet there's one kind of emotional attachment very common among working-class boys of the middle teens : a deep unquestioning friendship between two boys, founded on unshakable loyalty and interdependence which neither would recognize as "love" and which is summed up in the phrase "me and me mate." These friendships mean an absolute partenership and concurrence in everything, including sex : one of such a pair wouldn't think of masturbating "without me mate."

So there it is : in Britain, for the last century or two, two different social classes of boys have been growing through their adolescence in utterly different sexual and emotional atmospheres, among utterly different sexual and emotional ideas. Yet, from what I've seen of both systems, I believe that the liberalism in which the working-class adolescent grows up no more shapes his final sexual character than does purdah the upper-class boy's : both are fixed long before these contrasting environments are reached; but one can't doubt, I suppose, that the "natural" environment of the working-class adolescence must be emotionally healthier of the two.

*   *   *

There's another kind of adolescent purdah, the Italian. This separates the boys from the girls solely by a barrier of social punctilio, an inherited convention of "untouchability" which has acquired almost the force of the universal incest-taboo. It's a prohibition that's still rigidly observed in villages and small towns, though with the increasing liberalization of manners in the big cities, evasion of it is easy there. But in a village in southern Italy, boys and girls from puberty onwards may hardly look at each other, let alone stop for a chat, when they meet in the *piazza,* unless they are related by blood—even if they've been playing together since infancy. Throughout his adolescence a boy may not ever be alone with a girl; and even when, through the proper channels, he's proposed to and been accepted by the girl of his choice (or his parents'), he seldom can be alone with her unchaperoned, until the marriage. This archaic custom, which in a small town receives far more respect than any mere law of the land, preserves the *virgo intacta* rule : it's a measure of the fantastic value popularly attached to virginity in a bride—a broken maidenhead means no husband for the girl and social humiliation for her family. Also, in a south Italian community, parental watchfulness over their progeny's public behaviour, male or female, is that of a lynx; mainly to avoid reason for social disgrace, and partly to escape, should a son get some girl into trouble, the inevitable shotgun wedding with all the ignominy and disagreeable expense that this would bring. So what is the effect of this rigid convention on the adolescent boys?

The southern Italian boy has an abundant appetite for sexual pleasure, rarely for long assuaged. At some age between six and eight he begins to masturbate—anywhere along the seashore in summer one can see schools of such children working away at their infantile genitals : the act starts by being imitative—the latest six-year-old to join the group of course does what the others are doing—and instantly and naturally becomes a habit. Anywhere along the seashore in summer one will come upon the busy generation of sexual energy, and often its expenditure : a solitary boy, two or three together, a cluster—of all ages from near-infancy to late adolescence : the process goes on continually and follows every form one can think of—or rather, every form the boys can think of. Italian boys are sexually ingenious; and they are generally ready, provided they're given the active role, to do anything with almost anybody. They delight in sexual pleasure, for its own sake; and, because of the social taboo which governs their behaviour, the pleasure most of them yearn for stays inaccessibly and mysteriously out of their reach.

In nearly every village, and in nearly every *palazzo,* as any large block of dwellings is called in a small town, there's generally at least one teen-age girl who's lost her virginity and is ready to oblige any of the local adolescents for a consideration. A good many of the boys take advantage of this; but the job's not so simple as it sounds. There's the parental menace; and, also, a police menace—local police are always eager to watch the morals of the youngsters on their beat and supporting them are the laws protecting minors : a sixteen-year-old making love with a sixteen-year-old—both can be arraigned for under-age-corruption. And then there's money to be raised for the ten-minute assignation in some smelly doorway or other retreat; there's the competition of other boys of the *palazzo;* and, while one was waiting for her at some out-of-the-way spot, a film one wanted to see might be showing at the local cinema. Altogether, having the local tart was an expensive and tiresome and risky operation : masturbation was much simpler and safer; and masturbation, or other things, in the emotional company of one's friends gave one, really, just as much pleasure and none of the worry. In this way, almost every boy in southern Italy takes as a matter of course to homosexual activities in his adolescence, chiefly with his contemporaries in age but often with anybody else who offers not just money, but kindness and sympathy. Few Italians are wholly homosexual; but few aren't without at least a streak of it. Therefore, through the long purdah of their adolescence, most southern Italian boys get along contentedly with almost daily masturbation and a good deal of homosexual amusement with their friends—but homosexual only in deed : romantically, their eyes are forever roving over the girls of what's bureaucratically called their "age-group."

These boys, therefore, are cut off throughout their adolescence from girl-companionship, although they see girls every day—and girls whom they've known all their lives. But they mayn't look at them or speak to them; and so emotionally largely, and physically entirely, they're limited to the pleasures of their solitary erotic fantasies or the pleasures of physical experiment with their friends. And these are the things they do, and without stint. Yet nearly every southern Italian boy—I've hardly known one who didn't—when he gets into his twenties, marries a girl and begets a number of children; and continues generally to be a decent husband and a splendid father—there are no more doting fathers in the world.

*   *   *

And then there's the Arab brand of purdah, which inflexibly demarcates the entire human world into two distinct parts, the male and the female : two halves of living that meet only in the arcana of the family. But this is a very different purdah, being accompanied by an almost total sexual permissiveness which draws the line only at the deflowering of virgin girls. Otherwise the Arab boy or man may do what he likes, or what he can. The rich may keep a variety of women at home; for the poor there are generally brothels at hand, to which boys of quite tender age have access if they have enough money to pay. A man who is away from his own women and finds no others available will resort to boys—or even, in extremity, to animals (legend says that the pulpy interiors of melons are also used). The fact is that the average Arab—I'm speaking of the North African Arabs who are those I've lived amongst—needs any suitable orifice, uncomplicated by emotion : he wants sensation not romantic attachment, and he will use almost any means of obtaining that straightforward orgastic sensation. Among Arabs one finds an immense amount of homosexual behaviour but very little true homosexuality : the active partner wants a plain screw, not somebody to love; the passive, some benefit—money or other material advantage; some, no doubt, have to submit out of fear. This is the sexual attitude into which

boys grow up: the routine of family-building lies ahead—
two or three wives, perhaps, if one's lucky enough to be able
to afford them, plus even a handful of concubines; meanwhile
there's the brothel when one has the money, and any of one's
friends or smaller boys whom one can induce or seduce. Myth
too plays its part in the sexual *mors* of the Arabs: in
Morocco, for instance, pupils in the Koranic schools will
allow their teachers—who, being learned in the holy book, are
themselves holy—to bugger them because it's believed that
an injection of the holy semen quickens the ability to
memorize the Koran by heart (I'm writing of thirty years
ago: I don't know if this belief is still held). Again, in
Morocco, small boys in rural villages will copulate with the
female donkeys they look after because, legend says, this
encourages the growth of the penis.

So the Arab boy, almost still in infancy, quickly learns to
take practically any form of sexual activity as a matter of
course and to accept anybody—and even anything—as a
partner; and almost invariably he wants, as he grows up, to
perform the simple male role. He will, if required, simulate
an emotional interest and join in other modes of obtaining
pleasure—but what he really wants is the masterful thrust
from the haunches, getting his orgasm in the most male way
he can.

The Arab heart, I think, is lyrical rather than passionate;
he feels elegantly poetical about those who excite his amorous-
ness rather than profoundly emotional; his deepest feelings
are for his younger children. If in his household there's to be
found some beardless boy, he will be there as catamite, not as
beloved.

*   *   *

And what of those societies, which surely are in the
majority, in which no sort of purdah holds their adolescent
boys apart from their girls? What about, say, Japan? Or
Germany?

I suppose Japan is as permissive as any other country
today; I can recall no restrictions on the association of boys
with girls—certainly not in Tokyo, though I cannot speak
about rural communities where, perhaps, more squeamish
conventions may persist. But I believe that nobody who knows

the Japanese will demur when I say that homosexuality among them is noticeably frequent; and that, within that homosexuality, the love of men for boys and of boys for men exists on a wider front, perhaps, even than in Europe. It's true, certainly, that the Japanese, as a nation, are "neurotic" —a highly nervous, sensitive, overwrought people : a condition perhaps produced by their having packed into a few decades the mastering of technical skills and ingenuities which it had taken the West a couple of centuries to develop.

And Germany? I myself can say nothing about the Germany of today—I haven't been there since 1933. But in five years before that, when I lived there, boys were launched in early adolescence into a lushness of moral laxity which can't have been equalled since the "decadence" of the Roman Empire; "permissive" was indeed the word for German society in the 'twenties. Again, as in Japan much later, paedophilia was almost an accepted branch of social life, so widespread was it among boys as well as among men. Again, too, this was a period in Germany of acute "neurosis"—the aftermath of defeat in the war, of deprivations, of a riotous inflation and fearful unemployment. But who can say that a prevalence of paedophila and a nation's period of neurosis are in the least casually connected? Were the Greeks of the age of Pericles and Socrates neurotic?

Let's try another form of "permissive" society, and one that certainly wasn't neurotic at all : the Zulu nation as it was nearly fifty years ago, when I spent many months there, far "up country," among people still almost totally untouched by Western manners or morals, or even by the West at all. In these tribal, and kraal, societies, an absolute sexual permissiveness existed for adolescents of both sexes provided they stopped before penetration—here again the old, universal, primitive sanctity of the maidenhead was the rule, But, short of full copulation, anything was allowed : girls and boys just past puberty could go together into the bush—the woodlands surrounding their kraal or village—and do all the tricks they could think up. But penetration was taboo : a boy proved to have penetrated was banished from his kraal and tribe—and messengers sent to the neighbouring tribes asked that the guilty boy be rejected by them too. He became an outcast.

These people were pagans : they had their own strict moral

codes (one could leave one's hut open and everything in it, and nothing would be touched) which, once abrogated, left a vacuum. Young men in the kraals who felt it was time they had a bit of "penetration" too, would say to each other: "Let's go down to the mission station": and they'd set off over the bush tracks, brandishing their *assegais*, naked except for a figleaf of monkey's tails, and walk twenty miles to the nearest mission school, where Christianized girls, having lost their tribal taboos, were ready to accept "penetration."

But in the year or so that I lived among the Zulus, high on the uplands of Zululand northeast of Natal in South Africa, I never saw a sign of any kind of homosexual behaviour or understanding: not even among the boys—I never came across the slightest evidence of sexual play even among the smaller boys. Was this because these people were "primitive"? Because they were unaffected by Western neuroses?

But I've already described earlier in these pages another "primitive" African people—certainly, in Dakar, less "primitive" and for much longer and more closely susceptible to Western influence: I mean, of course, the people of Senegal, where society is as permissive as one can possible conceive it to be—I imagine there's nothing that any adolescent can't do, if he has a mind to do it (provided, of course, that he can obey the unalterable law, and pay for it). I don't think there's anything specially neurotic about the Senegalese; and Dakar, after all, has had two or three centuries of urban "civilization." And yet, though all is permitted to them, the Senegalese appear to be the queerest people in Africa— not excepting the Arab peoples of North Africa, where queerness is a pastime not an emotion.

*   *   *

I've put down here some of my observations, made in various parts of the globe. What can one make of them? I myself don't know. Trying to add them up doesn't seem to give a result.

My own conclusions, drawn from long decades of experience over a vast area of behaviour in a lot of countries, are unlikely to be confirmed by the psychiatrists—their profession depends largely on theories untested by experience "in the field," and is mystified by phraseology which nobody else wants to understand.

I believe it's true to say that most boys, during the two or three years after puberty, don't want to have girls, even if the girls are there to be had; and I believe that this is generally the rule whether they are kept in purdah or whether they're free to follow any sexual whim. Generally, I've observed, boys in their early adolescence prefer the companionship of other boys—they boast among themselves about what they'd do to a girl if they got one, although getting one is the last thing they want. Not until towards the age of seventeen (the age obviously isn't constant, just as the onset of adolescence itself varies with each individual) does a boy begin to need at least the companionship of a girl; at seventeen, generally, his emotional nature has reached the point of dichotomy and his inclinations have made themselves felt—his behaviour shows whether he is predominantly heterosexual or homosexual. I've recently—in the late 1960's—found additional evidence of this in London, where a great deal was being published about the new "permissiveness," innumerable "social surveys" revealing sensational details of sexual license among the young. But, I noticed, the boys one saw in the streets walking hand-in-hand with their "birds" were boys of eighteen or over, or perhaps of seventeen—but rarely of sixteen and almost never below that. The boys of fourteen and fifteen seemed to be amusing themselves in groups of their own kind, exactly as I'd always known them to do in the past; and weren't showing the slightest desire to have a "bird" in the tow of a sticky handclasp.

I believe it's true that adolescents of both sexes, before the sexual direction which their mature lives are going to take becomes differentiated—whether hetero or homo, or remarkably often both—tend to be homosexual during the year or two after puberty; there's evidence galore that lesbian behaviour is rife in girls' boarding schools—my own sister told me about her experiences. Boys in early adolescence most certainly become emotionally involved with their "mates," with or without sexual play together even though, partly to seem *à la mode,* they allow themselves romantic fantasies about idealized girls—a little in the manner, perhaps, of the medieval troubadours.

I believe that somewhere between the ages of sixteen and eighteen, say, the ultimate sexual and emotional shape of the boy's nature becomes set: after that his loves and his lusts will be "normal," or he will remain the homosexual he has mainly been so far. This rule, like so many others, is more often broken than not—simply because an amazingly high proportion of growing adolescents don't at all accomplish a true differentiation of their sexual natures and become hard-and-fast homosexuals or heterosexuals—they go into adulthood endowed with a very handy sexual ambivalence, able to have the best of both worlds. One cannot make a guess at the likely number of bisexuals in any community; but one's knowledge of friends and acquaintances shows that the percentage would astonish people unfamiliar with these matters.

I believe, again founding my belief on a lifetime of observation and experience, that the sexual differentiation that occurs about mid-adolescence or later and determines a person's emotional course through his life, isn't influenced by various environments of upbringing like purdah or the absence of it. And, I believe too, it isn't influenced in the slightest by sexual experiences in childhood or later, What, for instance, a homosexual environment (such as the purdah of the British public school, or initiation by "mates" or some fortuitous adult) obviously does is to provide opportunity, example, and experience which might never have come some particular youngster's way if he hadn't been introduced into that environment. But what surely it doesn't do, and I'm convinced *cannot* do, is alter the course of that differentiation when it occurs. Which branch the sexual nature takes at the bifurcation of adolescence has been fixed in infancy or, for all we know, before that; and I don't believe that any experience or environment or model can deflect, like switching the points on a railroad, from one branch to the other. Opportunity, a homosexual environment provides; and sometimes understanding—surely it's a good thing that a person should understand a puzzling nature? But what it can never create is appetite, when no appetite is there: nothing will give a taste for garlic in a mouth that dislikes garlic—certainly not shoving garlic into it. Nothing will make a homosexual of a nature that isn't already homosexual—certainly not inherently distasteful experience. And when a boy whose sexual course will later differentiate into perfect normality does have homosexual experience during his post-pubic "homo" years—the experience will run off him like water off a duck's back.

I have no theories; I have only experience. Experience tells me that education and example can change manners and attitudes but that nothing can change the nature, the personality, which makes every human being an individual.

NOTE ON NOMENCLATURE

The first three and last three paragraphs of this 'Note on Nomenclature' were omitted from the first edition.

For a long time I've felt the need for a note on nomenclature: for a scrutiny of the words English-speaking people use for that love which the Greeks called *paiderastia*—for the emotion a man feels when he's attracted by boys.

Language, of course, doesn't bother about producing a word for concepts which its speakers don't need; the Italians, for instance, do not understand or cherish personal privacy as we know and value it and therefore in Italian there's no real word for *privacy*. So far as I remember there's no word in Arabic for the Devil: *shitan*, Satan, is infinitely divisible, like a very low form of life, into an unending number of minute 'shitans' who go about doing mischievous things like tripping one up with a stone. But there's no word, I think, in the popular idiom for a single sovereign anti-God. African and Asian languages nowadays are necessarily packed with alien expressions to keep up with western ideas and techniques; modern Hebrew has had to invent a whole new vocabulary to cope with modern life.

But some languages, in some circumstances, go further than a merely passive neglect of little-needed notions; they aggressively refuse to name certain facts which their speakers prefer to reject as non-existent. This is especially true of

191

English, the language of a people particularly squeamish until recently about sexual actions and, still more so, sexual unorthodoxies. Thus, between the good old vulgar 'fuck' and the prissy and semi-academic 'copulate', English has nothing but a series of euphemisms—absurdities like 'going to bed with', as if one has to go to bed—to denote in polite speech or writing the ordinary coupling of men and women. Even in sub-polite language, euphemisms like 'screwing' are harsh and crude. For ordinary conversation, perhaps, 'have' is as agreeable and sensible as anything; the with-it modernism 'have it off' seems to give a schoolboyish, masturbatory sound.

It's not surprising, therefore, to find that English has refused point blank to provide a word for a man's love for boys, because the English refuse to admit that a man can love boys—and, what's more, that it puts every obstacle it can in the way of discovering a suitable word. Not so many decades ago all sexual heresies were lumped together as "unnatural vice" and none was allowed a word outside the "specialist" shelves of libraries. Gradually that hideous foreigner "homosexuality" has got itself accepted in "polite" circles, as well as intellectual; and the near-joke-word "lesbian" whirls about in drawing-rooms and on TV. (For a long time it was felt that if there *had* to be a word for something that ought never to be mentioned, then it should be a word which only an educated élite would understand.) Today it's become smart to use glib euphemisms like "queer," "bent," "camp" and "drag"—their comic slanginess vouches for their user's worldly understanding and also, by spreading a veneer of facetiousness over the nastiness of their meaning, gives him a complacent feeling of indulgent superiority.

But there's still no word for a man's love for boys, or for the love between boy and man. These things are today even further beyond the legal pale than they were before the "consenting adults" act of Parliament; and the English language cannot be brought to give it a name. We've had to make do with a noble Greek heirloom—"paederasty" and "paederast"; but unfortunately this heirloom has been debased by the malice of the language which, resenting its introduction, has given it a meaning wholly unjustified by the word's two Greek components. *The Concise Oxford Dic-*

tionary (1964 edition) curtly gives short shrift to the word: "*paederasty, ped-* n. Sodomy with a boy. So—*ast* n., sodomite." But the Greek word means neither less nor more than the plain meaning of its components: "love (or lover) of a boy"; and while the biblical report of the original sin of Sodom made no allegations of offences against boys, the Greek word "paederasty" by itself contains no motion of the act of sodomy. However, the word is no longer of use to lovers of boys—to paederasts; for "paederasty" has become almost the official euphemism for buggery in the criminal courts, a "paederast" in common parlance is a sodomite, and all its native emotion has gone out of the word. Some praiseworthy attempts have recently been made to find English equivalents of *paederastia,* an English attribute to define a man's sexual love for a boy or the sexual emotion that can exist between man and boy. "Boy-love" and "Greek love" seem almost to fill the bill; and yet I believe that neither will survive. The English language will reject them, not out of prejudice but because both are indigestible.

"Boy-love" won't do because it is ambiguous: English grammar, English idiom, and the logic or illogic of the English language refuse to make it other than ambiguous. Look at "boy-love" in any context you like, and see what you make of it. Does it mean a love for boys or the kind of love a boy feels—the emotion of a boy's love? To me, if it means anything at all, the second meaning comes out. But I'm inclined to think that, unless "boy" is an adjective qualifying "love" and thus meaning "boyish love," the term "boy-love" doesn't make sense at all. Probably the idea of using it came from the German "Knabenliebe"; but this is a false analogy: German, being an inflected language, enjoys a different and more precise way of composing words.

Let us look at some other words of the same sort of formation. "God-love"—what would that mean if it could exist? Or "God-fear," to try a different abstract noun? Not, surely, the fear of God? One talks, of course, about a dog-lover—just as one can say boy-lover; but what would "dog-love" mean? Surely, the kind of love felt by a dog. Woman-hater—but "woman-hate"? One might, at a stretch, make "woman-hatred" indicate a hatred of women, but it would require a good deal of mental contortionism and would draw a protest from grammar. One can think of two formations of this kind with "love" whose use is perfectly good and whose meanings are unequivocal : "calf-love" doesn't mean a love for calves, and "mother-love" means a mother's love for her child. No, "boy-love" won't do : the language refuses to have it. At its best it means the opposite of what's wanted in the present context; at its worst it means nothing. In between the two, it's always ambiguous.

"Greek love" won't do either; it can't last, I feel : not for grammatical reasons but for what one must call ideological ones. The fact that men's love for boys was socially approved, within limits, in classical Greece and became enshrined openly in a literature read throughout the educated world mainly because it's "classical," doesn't make anything that goes on in Brooklyn or Birmingham or Bergamo or Breslau or Besançon the slightest bit Greek; to expect it to, is rather like calling all food "French" because in France eating is a rite and not merely a chore. It seems to me as misconceived a straining after an apt generalization as is the old Italian definition of homosexuality as the "English vice"; and, on a very different level, as misplaced as the French jibe *capote anglaise* and the English tit-for-tat "french letter." Scotch whisky can't be made anywhere other than in Scotland, and therefore it's called "scotch" everywhere; but the love of boys thrives among peoples who've never heard of Greece. To apply to a ubiquitous emotion the attribute of a classical period in history and literature, seems to me like trying to cater for a narrow, rather snobbish "intellectual" cast. What the English-speaking boy-lovers of Puerto Rico, Singapore, Trinidad, Liverpool and a hundred other such places are to make of "Greek love," I don't know.

At the beginning of this century, after the Russian ballet of Diaghelev and Fokine had burst upon Europe, every little local company of dancers became a 'ballet' and every ballet called itself Russian. But within a decade or two all the European capitals and the big American cities had their national ballets, with the world's greatest dancers performing with them and the world's leading composers writing music for them. And the attribute 'Russian' withered away, or rather returned to its proper place, Russia's own native ballet. The dance, like love of all sorts, is universal; national

194

or historical adjectives have no right to behave like a general trade-mark.

But all this brings us no nearer to a word, or something less than a circumlocution, to cover the idea of a man's love for boys. None comes to mind; names stubbornly refuse to be invented, as if under the ban of the language. One may hope, perhaps, that some pop-philologist will find the answer.

For the time being we must still rely on the Greeks and be grateful for the beauty of the words theit liberality of language allowed them. We have seen that, for reasons of debasement by prejudice, we can't use 'paederast' or 'paederasty'—or, anglicised, 'pederast'. But there remains to us 'paedophilia' and 'paedophile': words as graceful as the others and meaning the same thing—although English dictionaries, for some reason, generally allow them a respectability now denied to the former. There can be nothing against giving them an English spelling and a workaday look; I don't think, though, I'd go as far as the Italians and turn the Greek *ph* into a Latin *f*—'pedofil' looks like something to do with bicycling. But I shouldn't mind being called a pedophil.

POSTSCRIPT

AN ENGLISH country squire who lived in the reign of the first Elizabeth wrote a lot of bucolic poetry in the manner of Virgil which was so good that much of it at one time was attributed to Shakespeare himself. His name was Richard Barnfield and many of his verses showed him to be an unabashed lover of boys. One of his best-known poems contains a couplet which, poetically feeble though it seems when read out of context, utters a profession of faith that every true boy-lover will echo —and by "true" I mean the paedophile who *loves* his boy-friend, finding his supreme pleasure in the boy's welfare and happiness. In these lines Barnfield said :

> If it be sin to love a lovely lad,
> Oh then sinne I, for whom my soul is sad . . . .

The rather lame sound, to modern ears, of the second line is surely deceptive : What the poet's saying, plainly, is that *if* loving a boy is, in the world's view and the Church's view, technically a sin, then he's sorry to be offending these views and sorry to committing what's officially a "sin"—but he knows jolly well in his own heart that his love is sinning against no one and neither affronts morality nor harms his beloved. *If* he's branded as a sinner—well, that's just too bad, but he's going on sinning with a clear conscience.

I've no apology to make for the matter of this book—I'm not now concerned with the manner of it. In Britain the sexual love of boys is one of the most grievous "sins" on the criminal and social score-sheet and, measured by the yardstick of prison sentences, has become more sinful than ever since homosexual behaviour between "consenting adults" was made legal by Parliament : legislative puritans rarely make concessions without requiring their *quid pro quo,* and their price for passing the homosexual bill was a statutory jump from a maximum of two years' imprisonment to ten for "indecent assault" on minors, consenting or not—a minor being somebody under 21. Not many years ago a British Judge, speaking from the Bench and therefore *ex cathedra,* pronounced the homosexual "corruption" of boys to be "worse than murder"—thus, off his own bat, contradicting Parliament, the authority that made the laws it was his job to administer : at that time Parliament still punished murder with hanging and "indecent assault" with up to two years in jail. Using the language and reasoning of the Middle Ages, this Judge declared : "The murderer only destroys the body; the corrupter of youth destroys the soul." Shortly after the "consenting adult" bill became law, the police in a British provincial town pounced on a small group of young homosexuals and prosecuted them—they were under 21 and therefore "minors"; one of these "criminals," aged 19, committed suicide before the actual trial began. And I heard recently— again since adult homosexuality was legalized—of a man found guilty of "indecent assault" who was imprisoned for *four years* for a first offence; before the "consenting adult" Act a first offender was generally placed on probation or at the most sentenced to four months.

Such is the temper in Britain, or at any rate the official temper and consequently the police temper; probably more widely, outside the incorruptible core of conformists to whom any kind of heresy is like a red rag to a bull, there's a less indignant attitude, a less obfuscated notion, especially now that "permissiveness" in nearly every other sphere of sexual eccentricity has become as commonplace as last week's Chelsea fashions. More and more permissive, no doubt, society generally will become; more and more tolerant and understanding, as in so many countries beyond Britain's insular shores, of other people's private emotional idiosyncracies; more and more aware that the adolescent's sexual and emotional growth is as natural and individual as his physical growth and as impossible to arrest or even control as his his innate taste and aptitudes. Yet the puritans and the prejudiced will never waver in their zeal to protect the sexual innocence of "our boys" : the age of consent for girls in Britain is 16; the new legal consenting age for boys will remain at 18 for a very long time. One cannot foresee in Britain the time when the paedophile will cease to be legally an outlaw and socially an outcast.

But the human race is too wide, human history too long and ancient, human nature too eclectic and human experience too veteran and too variegated, to be directed by the decisions of the British or any other Parliament or to obey what a consensus of tradition and convention and prejudice lays down as orthodox. A huge segment of humanity will always be heretic in a multitude of manners; the individual, thank God, is *individual*—that's what makes humanity interesting; how dull we should all be if the human race were an infinite reiteration of Sir Cyril Black !

A human act doesn't become a "sin" just because Parliament or St. Paul has said it is : only the conscience of the man who commits the act can decide in the light of what he believes whether it's morally right or wrong. The laws of social convenience, of course, are another matter—such as the laws for protection of property against theft or of the person against violence; but most of the sexual laws (except for those which regulate the family and safeguard progeny), the laws that is which seek to control legally the individual's profoundest emotional being, derive from nothing but some antique tradition, born mostly in the early Church, or from prejudices sprung from some frustration or convention or morbid and unhealthy fear. They have no social function.

My own conscience tells me, and has always told me, that love for a boy, provided that his welfare and happiness are paramount in the desires of the lover, cannot be a sin either against the boy or against society. Not that I should ever advocate or encourage paedophilia, if there were a choice to be made : were I able to deflect the emotional course of an incipient paedophile, I would vehemently counsel the direction of normality—not, certainly, for moral reasons but on grounds of social and even emotional convenience and for the sake of a greater likelihood of enduring sexual contentment. Ineffable happiness can be the reward on both sides of a generous love between man and boy; but by its own nature it is doomed to be ephemeral—although often succeeded by a lasting friendship, the magic of love must pass with the magic of boyhood. I repeat: although, after a mainly happy life-time, I don't for a moment wish that I'd been born sexually different from what I was, I would always try to dissuade, were it possible to alter an individual nature, a youth from obeying an inclination toward boys— if he could bring him-self to disobey it; not because I believe his love would neces-sarily do harm to a boy (of course, there *are* expressions of this kind of love, as of any other, that can be harmful) but because his only chances of emotional serenity are almost certain to be wrecked by it. I don't believe a man's love can harm a boy morally or emotionally, so long as it's a tender gentle love whose principal concern is the boy's happiness and well-being; a love, that is, where the lover's principal pleasure is the advancement of the boy's happiness. What on earth or in heaven, in these circumstances, can some simple and passionate embrace matter?

Encouraged by dogmatic pronouncements from the magi-sterial bench, and by the lurid stories of depravity which the popular newspapers delight to tell in tones of outraged virtue, most people among the uninformed and the intolerant believe the boy-lover to be a specially nasty kind of sex-maniac who satisfies his unspeakable lusts by violence, deceit and "cor-ruption" and whose aim in life is buggery. Long experience of paedophilia and acquaintance with a large number of paedophiles have convinced me, on the contrary, that active buggery, and even the desire for it, are rare among true boy-lovers (though frequent among the pseudo-queers, like the Arabs) and that very, very rarely is an adolescent boy in-clined to accept a passive part in it. The true paedphile, even in his treatment of casual, fly-by-night "trade," is gentle, caressing and solicitous: he won't do, nor try to do, anything that the boy doesn't himself want to do.

The general public are also constantly told by the spokes-men of the "establishment"—judges, police-employed psy-chologists, prison-doctors, and the like—to believe that homo-sexual experience creates a taste for homosexuality among the young—that it's "catching" like the measles (these magistrates and others conveniently forget their own schoolboy experi-ences). The truth obviously is that a homosexual environment, or association with paedophiles, provides the *opportunity* for homosexual adventure which must often be eagerly grasped by young people who are by nature homosexually inclined—an opportunity that surely may be beneficial where lack of it can only mean the morbid smothering of a constitutional desire, but which can never change a sexual nature that is constitutionally antipathetic to homosexuality. Anyone who's seen something of adolescent sexuality knows that seduction into homosexual practices of a young "normal" isn't going to divert him subsequently from his need for normal sex. (That seduction by bribery may sow the seeds of prostitution is obviously true; but this is a problem within the much wider context of sexual commercialism generally. No one, surely, will want to deny that every time a man offers payment to a boy or young girl for any sort of sexual service, he's helping to equate sex with money in that young mind and nobody will want to doubt that this is harmful—because it degrades the emotions of sex.)

I've never heard that any of these publicists of the "contagiousness" of homosexuality has put forward some proof in support of his assertion—it remains a theory; whereas the paederastic practitioner finds ample proof in his own physical experiences and emotional relationships that no amount of homosexual play will or can deflect an amatorially normal boy from his heterosexual destiny. To such a boy a physical affair with another male is merely a substitute, an emotional pretence in the image of the "real thing"; or else it's a variation on the theme of masturbation. Naturally, as has been suggested above, there's any amount of proof to show that the greater the homosexual *opportunity* the more frequent is homosexual *practice*—this is the same thing as saying that the longer the pubs are open the more beer will be drunk; but it's a statement that has no bearing on the argument whether the heterosexual temperament can or can't be perverted on to a homosexual course.

I've known many boys in my time, and have loved a number of them. I don't believe I've done any real harm to any of them, and certainly none at all to those I loved; to most of those last, indeed, I know I did good—and not only material good; from some of them in later life I received their own testimony. Obviously, all my relationships with boys haven't been blameless—I must, I'm afraid, have disappointed or helplessly deceived or in some way emotionally wounded several: often some sad, pleading face gazes pitiably at me from some far-off scene in the past; and besides, I'm ashamed to say, in the minds of many others over the decades I must have helped to bedevil the idea of sexual pleasure with that of commercial gain. This is evil.

But perhaps the greatest harm I've done has been where I'd hoped to do most good and where love often was truest. This has happened not by my own volition but because of the worldly brutalities—the crass compulsions of displacement which, when one's life is a peripatetic one, can with the abruptness of a typhoon pick one out of a haven of happiness and buffet one a thousand miles into another world. That's where I've done harm; I've given comfort and prosperity and contentment and hope to a boy who has entrusted me with his security—and then, by neither my wish nor my fault, have betrayed that trust. Now and then, in one part of the globe or another, I've lifted a boy up to a level of security he'd never dreamed of, and then been forced by the cruel dictates of circumstances to leave him to topple off again. These are the episodes I look back upon with shame and sorrow, and with anger at myself.

I've done my best to leave a boy happier than I found him. Of course sometimes I've failed; of course often I've been beastly—selfish, thoughtless, perhaps unwittingly cruel. What harm I've done has been the fault of my own character or of the wilfulness of life—never of love itself and its little accessory embraces.

Some other titles in our series of Memoirs by gay men are:

Michael Davidson

THE WORLD, THE FLESH AND MYSELF

Introduced by Colin Spencer

Michael Davidson was a widely respected foreign correspon-
dent. He joined the Berlin communists against Hitler, crossed
wartime Morocco in disguise, and campaigned against British
oppression in Malaya and Cyprus. He was also imprisoned for
his sexuality. This celebrated autobiography is now published
for the first time with the author's annotations and photographs.

Described by its author as "the life story of a lover of boys",
this book has also been hailed by Arthur Koestler as "the
courageous and lovable story of a brilliant journalist's strug-
gles", and by James Cameron as "one of the best evocations of
the period that I know".

"More than welcome . . . narrated with the rage and wit of
complete sanity" (*New Statesman*).

ISBN 0 907040 63 2 (pbk)
ISBN 0 907040 64 0 (hbk)

The Erotic World of Peter de Rome

by Peter de Rome

This English film-maker, resident in America, won fame for his films described as "an elevated celebration of sex" (*Financial Times*).

Witty and adventurous, de Rome's own life reads like the screenplay for one of his films, taking him through the wartime RAF, New York in the 1950s, the Civil Rights movement in the Deep South, as well as the story of his movies.

"De Rome's racy literary style should ensure him a wide readership" (*Gay Times*).

ISBN 0 907040 46 2

Parallel Lives

by Peter Burton

Among the topics covered in this crowded memoir are the mod clubs of the 1960s; a teenage literary apprenticeship; collaborations with Robin Maugham; reminiscences of Gerald Hamilton ("Mr Norris") and Michael Davidson; touring with Rod Stewart; and the rise and fall of *Gay News*.

"As a social historian he is completely to be trusted. As a human being he is extremely sympathetic" (George Melly, *New Society*). "I am charmed by it" (*New York Native*).

ISBN 0 907040 65 9

Teardrops On My Drum

by Jack Robinson

Liverpool in the 1920s: still Dickensian in its poverty, a city of docklands and back alleys, barefoot kids running wild in the filthy streets, bizarre eccentrics and sectarian violence. This is the world marvellously evoked by Jack Robinson in the story of his boyhood: forced to fend for himself from the earliest age, searching the city for adventure, love and sex, and joining the army as a 14-year-old boy soldier.

  'A fascinating autobiography with its evocative descriptions of life in the Liverpool of the 1920s' *(Time Out)*.
ISBN 0-85449-003-5

Jack and jamie Go To War

by Jack Robinson

This second volume starts in 1937, with the fifteen-year-old hero back in his home town after his spell as a boy soldier. The action ranges from Liverpool under the Blitz through D-Day,, via New York, South Africa, and the Allied landings in Naples. It sees Jack as a wartime commando, then a seaman with the convoys, caught up in mutiny and racketeering, and always in pursuit of boys.
ISBN 0 85449 077 9

GMP books can be ordered from any bookshop in the UK, and from specialised bookshops overseas. If you prefer to order by mail, please send full retail price plus £1.00 for postage and packing to GMP Publishers Ltd (M.O.), P O Box 247, London N15 6RW. (For Access/Eurocard/Mastercharge give number and signature.) Comprehensive mail-order catalogue free on request.

In North America order from Alyson Publications Inc., 40 Plympton St, Boston, MA 02118, USA.

****

PLEASE SEND MAIL-ORDER CATALOGUE TO:

Name..

Address ....

....

....

....